GROW YOUR
GEEKS

A Handbook for Developing Leaders in High-Tech Organisations

ANTOINETTE OGLETHORPE

Praise

"Clear, engaging and practical, this book is a 'must read' for Senior Leaders and HR partners alike, in fast growing high-tech environments. A major challenge in such a competitive arena is attracting, acquiring and retaining the brightest talent. This book truly identifies the equal challenge in developing those bright, driven and highly technical people into the leaders needed to support and sustain continued growth."

Bernice Leppard, HR Director, UK, Nordics & MENA, BravoSolution

"*Grow Your Geeks* represents great guidance from a top quality business coach. More than a book, it is a business focused coaching programme designed for tech business leaders who need to translate the development of their leaders into continued business success. There is value-add from the very start and it hits the nail on the head with regard to the key leadership challenges facing fast moving hi-tech companies. It goes on to offer a structured method and approach that is very practical and easy to follow with a minimal amount of 'fluffy' psychobabble. A fantastic and highly-recommended resource."

Sue Holly-Rodway, Senior Director UKI, Oracle Corporation

"This is an insightful and entirely practical handbook for modern management to nurture and make successful the next generation of technology leaders. Based on real-world experience of the author rather than dry management science, the tools and techniques described are easily implemented and effective to help identify and grow those who will envision and create the future."

Mark Taylor, VP, Oracle Corporation

"This is a great book that helps answer many of the questions that companies battle with as they grow and need leaders to grow with them. Antoinette does a great job in discussing the differences between a 'leader' and a 'manager' and what strategy you should pursue for your company. This book shows you how the person answering the phone can be a leader in their own little domain if the right learning culture is in place to drive sustainable growth. This book will help you define it."

John Fallou, CEO, Unio Corporation

"This is a highly actionable leadership development bible, applied in the context of the challenges and opportunities of the high growth tech sector. It is definitely something I will go back to for ideas and guidance over and over again."

Ruth Bowen, Sales & Leadership Development Specialist, Veritas Technologies Ltd

"This book is written in a very accessible style, underpinned by a practical and robust six-step system, which will clearly enable the development of leaders. The insightful questions which appear throughout the book, are borne of significant experience and provide structure and a framework for implementation."

Professor Jane Turner, Pro-Vice-Chancellor, Teesside University

"Thought this book was excellent. Extremely readable, clear and packed full of practical advice. Many (if not most) people are promoted to a leadership role with little or no guidance, so this is an essential reference point from an industry expert. From the pristine new manager to the experienced old warhorse, there are lessons here for everybody and (surprisingly) every industry. I'm going to use the tips with my team – and I'm not even in the technology sector! Highly recommended!"

Dr Rikki Bhatia, Service Excellence Leader

"A commonsense book offering practical tips for growing your leaders (not just your geeks in my opinion!). An easy read which is all in plain English (refreshingly there is *no* jargon!) and logically laid out with provocative questions to help shape your thinking, summaries for easy reference and action points to help you plan for the future. This is the kind of book that I know will be a valuable addition to my bookshelf and one that I will dip into regularly in my work."

Abigail East, Director & Consultant, Effectus People Solutions

RƎTHINK PRESS

First published in Great Britain 2017
by Rethink Press (www.rethinkpress.com)

© Copyright Antoinette Oglethorpe

Contents

Chapter Five

Chapter Six

This book is about helping people realise their potential. It is dedicated to the people in my life who help me realise mine.

For Dave, my husband, my partner and my best friend. Where you lead, I will follow.

For all my deeply loveable, highly entertaining and perhaps just slightly eccentric close family.

Introduction

The single biggest way to impact an organization is to focus on leadership development. There is almost no limit to the potential of an organization that recruits good people, raises them up as leaders and continually develops them.

JOHN C MAXWELL

The High-tech Sector in the UK has grown by the equivalent of one new business every hour for the last five years.[1] But these fast-growing companies face unique challenges. There are the pressures of constant change, the urgency of speed to market, the risk of uncertainty and the demand for agility.

If you're a leader of a high-tech company I have good news and I have bad news. The good news is the Tech Sector is still in good health and there is plenty to smile about. The bad news is that a shortage of leaders could stop you from growing any further.

High-tech companies attract the best and brightest people who are driven by ambition and individual achievements. There was a time when being a 'geek' meant you were boring,

---

1   KPMG (Dec 2015), 'Tech Monitor'

square, as far as you could get from being 'cool'. Now, geeks have the potential to rule the world. Geek *is* cool. Dare I say, geek is chic.

But geeks may not be seasoned, proven leaders. And that's a problem.

Having strong leadership and skilled, motivated employees is critical for the successful growth and competition of any tech company.[2] Perhaps more so than for any other type of business.

As Steve Jobs said, 'To turn really interesting ideas and fledgling technologies into a company that can continue to innovate for years requires a lot of disciplines.'

The demands placed on people in fast-growing and high-tech companies are significant. They include the following:

❯ The rate and pace of change
❯ The complexity of integrating different systems, processes and applications, which often result in major outages and instability issues
❯ An ongoing need to innovate
❯ Threats to the business, particularly cyber security and privacy-related issues
❯ Gaining and retaining competitive advantage through technology and information systems
❯ Anticipating and responding to client demands.

Without good leadership and proper support, employees can become overstretched and under motivated. All too often, good people burn out and leave.

---

2   Culture Amp (2016), 'New Tech – Benchmark Report'

High-tech companies are hugely dependent on the creativity, productivity and dedication of their staff. It has never been so easy for staff to find other jobs and move to other companies. The 'war for talent' is real in the High-tech Sector.

The big question is 'How can you develop leaders who can keep up with and drive the growth of your business to ensure long-term success?'

That's what I've designed this book to answer.

Who this book is for

This book is for busy leaders and HR professionals in fast-growing high-tech companies. Your company has probably grown quickly because you've got brilliant technologies and products.

But you're in danger of getting stuck because you don't have enough leaders with the skills and confidence to grow the business further. You're finding it hard to develop leaders, keep them engaged and create a culture for innovation that fuels future growth.

Leadership development is an important part of a company's 'growing up' process. In *Grow Your Geeks* I'll show you how to develop more and better leaders. I'll show you how to enable your leaders so they have the confidence to make decisions and take action. And I'll show you how to get your leaders to take ownership of leading people and the organisation. This book will help you develop the leadership capacity, capability and culture that you need to deliver fast, sustainable growth.

I'm going to share with you the practical six-step LEADER system I've developed during my years of experience working with high-tech companies. I'm going to give you the practical tools and techniques to answer fundamental questions:

- ❯ What are the critical skills that leaders of fast-growing high-tech companies need to succeed?
- ❯ How do we recruit, keep and develop the right people in a competitive high-tech market?
- ❯ How do we test the capacity and capability of current leaders to scale with future growth?
- ❯ How can we ensure that an employee with great technical skills will be a great leader or manager?
- ❯ How do we give people the support they need to enable them to perform at their best?
- ❯ How do we develop agile career paths that give people the opportunities they're looking for so they stay with the company?
- ❯ How do we build the ability to innovate and respond to changing technologies and markets?
- ❯ How do we create a culture of growth that everyone buys into?
- ❯ How do we preserve the positives of the company culture as we grow?

This system didn't hit me like a lightning bolt. It came through countless hands-on experiences, and I've been refining it, one lesson at a time, in the real world for over twenty-five years.

And I'm still learning.

Grow Your Geeks step by step

In picking up this book you've shown commitment to developing your leaders. Now I need you to be honest with yourself. I need you to be willing to invest the time and effort to make the changes and reap the rewards.

In Chapter One we'll look at why leadership development is important to high-tech companies. Then we'll get into the detail of the LEADER system.

L is for Level

The Level step looks at where your leadership development is today – and where it needs to be for your company's growth.

E is for Envisage

Once you know what you want to change and the benefits of doing so, you're better able to envisage what your leaders need to do. And you can identify how they need to behave to deliver the business strategy. Envisage defines the leadership roles, skills and behaviours your company needs for the future.

A is for Assess

Once you've defined what successful leadership means for your company, you'll want to assess the readiness of your potential leaders to take on new roles and responsibilities.

You need to assess that readiness from two perspectives – the organisation's and the employee's.

D is for Develop

During the Assess stage you will agree the development areas for each individual. In the Develop stage you will focus on addressing those areas. You will develop the skills, behaviours and confidence of your future leaders.

E is for Embed

Developing leadership within your organisation means changing people's behaviour. The Embed component focuses on how you embed new leadership behaviours in the workplace to improve leadership on a day-to-day basis.

R is for Reinforce

As leaders develop new skills and behaviours, it will become clear that some aspects of the organisation will need to change to reinforce and support those new behaviours.

My story

Who am I to tell you how to develop your leaders?

During my years in business I have developed leaders for some of the most successful organisations in the world. I started my career in research and development for P&G, and I quickly discovered I was more interested in developing people than washing powders. That was where my passion for leadership development first started. I've never looked back.

Since then I have helped develop thousands of leaders for companies like Accenture, XL Group and Saint-Gobain.

More importantly, I've been a leader and an HR professional in a fast-growing high-tech company, Avanade, a joint venture between Accenture and Microsoft. It was formed in the year 2000 at the height of the dot-com boom. Tech companies were springing up everywhere – it was the birth of Silicon Valley. Twenty-year-old geeks who couldn't get a date in school were starting companies in their bedrooms, becoming millionaires overnight.

Among the crowd of start-ups, Avanade was different. For one, it was the brainchild of two well established, successful companies. And secondly, it was global. Avanade started up in eleven countries all at the same time.

But it faced the same challenges as every other start-up. It needed brilliant products and services that solved genuine client problems. It needed people – and lots of them – to deliver those products and services and solve those client problems. And it needed to do that in a way that it could grow and scale quickly.

The company needed the technical skills, consulting skills and management skills to serve clients. As International Training Director, my brief was clear: I was responsible for developing the workforce in every country outside the US. It wasn't long before I got my British Airways Gold Card as I travelled the world, putting the learning and development operation in place.

In twelve months, we had grown the company to over 1,200 employees working in the US, Europe, Asia and Australia. Although in a global role, I was in the UK – a country in which the company's growth was the fastest outside the US. We heralded our wins and welcomed yet more new employees to our growing company. At a party for the company's birthday (which was coincidentally the same day as my own), I stood next to the General Manager, surveying the bar full of our employees, looking in wonder at what we'd achieved and feeling so proud. It was like we were part of one big, happy family, working together and making a difference.

Then the dot-com bubble burst. And everything changed.

Having set up the learning and development operation everywhere outside the US, I had been asked by the company to take on the role of HR Director for the UK. In my first day in the role, the General Manager invited me out for a drink. *How kind*, I thought. *It's to welcome me to his leadership team.*

Well, yes, it was. And it wasn't.

Over my 'welcome' drink, he told me that my first task as HR Director was to make 10% of the workforce redundant. The UK had grown so quickly that we had too many consultants and not enough client projects. Eleven people had to go.

I don't think it matters how logical, commercial or business minded you are, when you have someone's career in your hands, it is a heart-wrenching, stomach-churning feeling. I will never forget standing in the Boardroom the day the General Manager told those eleven people their jobs were at risk. One young man's head fell to the desk in despair. He had just exchanged contracts on his first house.

And the atmosphere in the company changed. We weren't a big, happy family any more. We were 'them' and 'us' – the management who could take jobs away, and the employees who had delivered all the work but could still be let go at a moment's notice.

As HR Director, my brief now was to rebuild morale. I needed to develop a workforce that would not only survive but thrive through the downturn.

We had grown so far on technical know-how. Now we needed more know-what and know-who. We needed good, strong leaders, and we needed them to have the skills and confidence to take action. We needed to develop that culture throughout the organisation.

I learned a lot through that period. I learned that you need leaders at every level of the organisation if you are going to grow sustainably; you need to focus on the future success you want to create rather than the past that you want to change; you need to envisage the future and identify the leaders to realise that vision.

I learned that not all employees have the potential or ambition to take on leadership roles. You need to assess their ability and their motivation. I learned that people don't develop leadership skills and confidence by osmosis. You need to develop your current and future leaders proactively. I learned that if you want leadership to become part of the fabric of your organisation, you need mechanisms in place: processes and practices that will embed and reinforce the correct behaviours daily.

In his book *Outliers*, Malcolm Gladwell repeats the generally accepted wisdom that it can take 10,000 hours to become an expert in any field. There are plenty who dispute that theory, but it's safe to say that it takes time to accumulate knowledge and experience. Having spent over twenty-five years working in the field of leadership development, I've clocked up many more than 10,000 hours.

When I first meet clients, it's clear that they too are experts. But while they are leaders in their field, their field is not leadership. And they don't know where to start when it comes to developing the leaders they need to grow the business.

That shouldn't be a surprise. One of the great things about the High-tech Sector is that progress happens rapidly. Someone can go from student to CEO of a highly capitalised company in two years. That is completely different from years ago, when progressive promotion was the order of the day. But it does mean that people at the top of high-tech organisations often are not experienced in leadership themselves, let alone experienced at developing other leaders.

I know how confusing it can be. Anything to do with developing leaders seems overcomplicated with management speak and cumbersome HR processes. And I've discovered that those corporate approaches aren't agile enough for a fast-moving organisation.

That's why I translated my experience into a practical six-step system and built a roadmap for keeping and developing leaders that you can use in your organisation.

It takes investment, effort and skilful application. But if you're committed to developing your leaders, you will make it work.

How to use this book

You can use this book in one of two ways. You can read it through from start to finish to get a complete overview of the LEADER system. Or you can use it as a reference book, dipping into the relevant sections as you're focusing on different stages of the framework.

My suggestion is that you do both. Read it through, make notes on the areas you think are most relevant to you and your company, then take action and come back to review when needed.

Many ideas in the book will make sense when you read them. But they won't make any difference until you apply them in your company.

At the end of every chapter you'll find a summary of the main points and a list of suggested actions to make your leadership development more effective. To help you put the ideas into practice, I've created some free resources, templates and checklists that you can use.

Go to www.antoinetteoglethorpe.com/grow-your-geeks-resources and register to access.

So let's get started. Let's look at how the LEADER system can help you.

Chapter One

Leadership Development

I'll bet most of the companies that are in life-or-death battles got into that kind of trouble because they didn't pay enough attention to developing their leaders.

WAYNE CALLOWAY,
former Chairman, PepsiCo Inc.

Here's the bottom line: companies which don't invest in developing their leaders make less than half the revenue per employee compared to those which do.[1] Those same companies deliver shareholder returns that are 22% lower.[2] The companies' value can be reduced by as much as 30%.[3]

In this chapter I will help you understand why leadership development is critical if you want to sustain fast growth of an organisation. I'll share with you the three biggest leadership challenges facing fast-growing high-tech organisations, introducing you to five principles to

---

1   Bersin (2010), 'Talent Management Factbook'
2   McKinsey (2001), 'War for Talent Studies'
3   Watson Wyatt (2005), 'Human Capital Index'

follow when developing leaders. I will encourage you to reflect on how you currently develop leaders in your organisation.

Why leadership development is critical

Despite an uncertain economy, political issues around the world and competition increasing on a daily basis, technology companies continue to deliver growth and create jobs. Importantly, they are optimistic about the future.

> *Since the end of the financial crisis, we have seen a UK Tech Sector that has delivered six years of continuous growth and created jobs at a faster and higher rate than the rest of the UK economy.*
>
> KPMG TECH MONITOR

The High-tech Sector has supported a massive increase in the number of digital start-ups and has been a source of many successful fast-growing scale-up companies. The number of high-tech companies has risen by a third since 2010, which is twice the level of growth for all private sector enterprises.

IBM studies reveal that over 70% of CEOs say employees are their primary source of sustainable economic value. Yet most organisations lack the skills they need to compete, and that's affecting business. Research by Accenture shows that 66% of companies expect to lose business because of talent gaps.

Engagement is also an issue.[4] Disengaged workers continue to outnumber engaged workers. In the UK alone, actively disengaged employees cost the country between £52 billion and £70 billion per year.[5] It's not surprising that 83% of companies are worried about their leadership pipelines.

That's a danger for high-tech companies that want to continue to grow.

Strong leadership and skilled, motivated employees are critical for the growth of any company. There aren't many other businesses that evolve as quickly as the High-tech Sector, and that can create unique challenges.

One example that is distinctive is the need for leaders to really know their employees. As the High-tech Sector changes, there will always be a group of employees who want to learn about the latest tools. Leaders need to keep them at the forefront of the developments so that they stay engaged. But there will be other employees who tire of always having to learn new technologies. Instead, they want to focus on the business aspect of technology delivery. It's important for leaders to know how to manage both types of people. They need the right blend of staff to keep the business tech savvy as well as business-focused.

High-tech companies can no longer leave that to chance and hope that their employees are as engaged as they want to be. The competition for talent in the tech sector is fierce...and employees know it.

---

4   Deloitte (2014), 'Global Human Capital Trends 2014: Engaging the 21st Century Workforce'
5   Gallup (2012), 'State of the Global Workplace: Employee Engagement Insights for Business Leaders Worldwide'

Research shows that employees in the High-tech Sector are more positive about their companies than those in other industries.[6] In particular, they are more likely to recommend their company as a great place to work and are more motivated to put in extra effort. They may not be looking for another job right now, but they are not necessarily committed to staying with their company in the medium to long term.

To compete, tech companies need a business-led leadership development strategy.

The three biggest leadership challenges

The fast-paced environment in which they thrive leaves many high-tech companies facing three key leadership challenges. I call them the Three Cs – Capacity, Capability and Culture.

1. Capacity

If an organisation is to grow, it needs the right people and the right leadership. A shortage of leaders at every level is the biggest challenge to the organisation sustaining growth, even if it can create client demand.

Consider the scenario of a company where the local market is developing rapidly. Many would consider it to be in a lucky position with clients clamouring for its products and services. But with a lack of leadership capacity comes the risk of not delivering. And in a competitive market, a reputation for poor delivery is almost worse than a lack of demand.

---

6   Culture Amp (2015), New Tech Benchmark Report.

In the words of one of my clients, 'We have increasingly been able to build our demand, but ensuring we have the right people to deliver on this demand is really tough. There are brilliant potential employees, but understanding what leaders we need and how to get people up and running quickly, effectively and productively is our biggest challenge.'

2. Capability

Companies are also struggling with leaders lacking the critical skills they need to succeed.

Employees in the technology sector are intelligent, educated and innovative. And they're used to thinking about the world in digital terms and on a global scale. In a fast-growing technology company, talented employees often fast-track through promotions. Their innovative skills and abilities take root and bear profitable fruit. But there's little chance to instil the foundations of the leadership needed to continue growth. They may have had limited exposure to management and leadership positions. That means they lack skills, experience and confidence in leading themselves, others and the organisation.

Take one of my clients, for example, which is a fast-growing technology consultancy with seventeen global offices across twelve countries. Employees work on different projects for different clients. The project managers manage them on a day-to-day basis to deliver what the client needs, so each employee might work for several different managers during a twelve-month period. This approach works well from an operational perspective, but it is short-term and can be unsettling for employees. They can feel that there is no-one looking out for them as individuals and helping them develop their career.

When a consultancy is small, this approach works. But as the company grows, it's no longer workable for the management team to manage everyone.

That's what happened with my client. The staff survey showed employees were uncertain what the future held for them. They felt they lacked recognition and development. And they didn't know what they needed to do to progress.

So the company introduced a role that would be responsible for focusing on the individual, which is what most consultancies do when they grow beyond a certain size. The person in this role is responsible for keeping regular contact with named employees. They're responsible for managing the performance of those employees across the different projects they work on and supporting their career development within the organisation. Those responsibilities need new skills and behaviours, and the new managers had limited experience.

I spoke to each of the managers about what they might need to develop. The overriding theme of their responses was that they are committed to the people they're managing and want to do right by them.

As one of them said, 'I don't want to be "just a manager", I want to be a good manager.'

They recognised that their people are all different, realising that meant they needed to adapt their style, but they were unsure how to do that. And they were anxious about dealing with the tough stuff and having difficult conversations.

One manager said, 'It's easy when everything's going OK. But what about when things go wrong?'

Fast-growing high-tech companies face an urgent need to develop leaders at all levels. They need to bring young leaders on faster, develop leaders globally, keep senior leaders engaged and build new leadership pipelines at every level of the company.

3. Culture

Building leaders requires more than a portfolio of training programmes. It means having a culture of growth that everyone buys into to broaden the opportunity for leaders to develop in new ways. This means putting potential leaders in positions that stretch them beyond their current skill sets, coaching and supporting them so they build their capabilities rapidly.

Fast-growing companies also face the challenge of preserving the positives of their culture as they grow. I know from my experience at Avanade that company culture is generally formed early on by founding members and key management. These individuals work closely together, making it relatively easy to maintain company culture. But as the company adds new personalities (not to mention extra locations), it can be a real challenge to assimilate all these individuals and preserve the company culture.

One of my clients made a good point. He said, 'We pride ourselves in having a good culture in the company and we talk about how can we preserve that when we're growing, but personally I believe that culture is very much a reflection of the people in your organisation. That makes culture a living thing: a living organism that will change over time with the number of people and the teams that you put in place. The culture needs to mature and evolve too.'

3 BIGGEST LEADERSHIP CHALLENGES

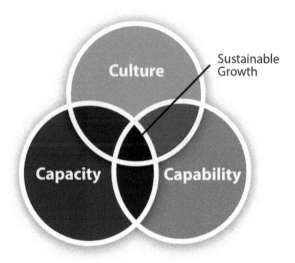

For sustainable growth you need all three Cs. Having only two of the three will leave you vulnerable in different ways.

For example, if you have enough leaders (capacity) with the skills and confidence to lead the business (capability) but you lack the processes and practices to reinforce leadership throughout the organisation (culture), you might be fine in the short-term, but leadership will be limited to the current leaders and you won't be able to sustain that leadership as you grow.

If, on the other hand, you have leadership capacity and a strong leadership culture but those leaders lack the skills to lead a fast-moving high-tech company, there is likely to be in-fighting, friction and resentment among colleagues as the business struggles to deliver in the face of high demand. And you will be vulnerable to attack by competitors. If you lack leadership capability, you will be too busy focusing on the day-to-day tasks and activities to concentrate on strategy for future growth.

Finally, if you have capable leaders and a strong leadership culture but you lack capacity, you run the risk of not being agile and responsive. You might be overflowing with ideas, but not have enough leaders to recruit and manage the teams to capture the good ones before the competition does.

Five guiding principles for effective leadership development

How can you develop the confident and skilful leaders your company needs for its continued growth and success? How can you do it in a way that is dynamic and reflects the pace of the sector it serves? How can you turn a 'box to be ticked' into an enjoyable experience that forms the foundations of success?

The best way to cultivate the mindset you need is through a set of principles to guide you as you design and put in place your leadership development strategy.

1: Leadership is a responsibility

People often confuse leadership with a role or position. But whether you're the CEO, a Director, or a Manager, your title will not make you a leader. Some of the worst leaders I have ever met have had the grandest job titles. Equally, there is no reason why you can't be a leader without a specific position or job title.

Leadership is a responsibility. It's all about making things happen, walking the talk, achieving the objectives and, above all, making a difference. You need all employees to do that.

Too many companies confine their leadership development efforts to senior individuals. But you can't afford to leave leadership up to those few individuals at the top of the organisation. Not if your company is going to grow quickly and be successful.

That is not to say senior executives don't have a part to play. They do. But position simply determines the *scope* of your leadership influence.

Obviously, the greatest influence is at the top of the organisation. People in senior positions are responsible for leading the whole organisation. Mid-level leaders are responsible for leading others in functions and project teams. Front-line employees and sole contributors may not lead and manage others, but they still need to lead themselves to increase their personal effectiveness and performance.

You need every employee to establish a shared vision, help get buy-in and influence direction, and motivate and inspire others.

2: Leadership is contextual

Contrary to popular belief, there is no single definition of what makes a great leader. A brilliant leader in one situation does not necessarily perform well in another. Academic studies have shown this, and my experience bears it out.

Take, for example, Marissa Mayer, the last CEO of Yahoo. Mayer's hiring in July 2012 was heralded as a coup for the struggling company, which was in a state of turmoil at the time and had run through four chief executives in the previous four years. It had poached Mayer from a high-profile role at Google, where she was credited with key contributions to many of the company's most important products. But Yahoo, with its years-long profits slump, had a different set of challenges to Google. For four years, Mayer attempted to turn around Yahoo's fortunes, but to no avail. Instead, Yahoo was sold to Verizon for $5bn.

Too many training programmes I come across rest on the assumption that one size fits all. They assume the same group of skills or style of leadership is suitable regardless of strategy or organisational culture.

When developing leaders, fast-growing high-tech companies need to ask themselves, 'What, precisely, are we developing leaders for?' The answer will determine the kind of leaders you need.

For example, if the answer is to support an acquisition-led growth strategy, you will need leaders brimming with ideas who can devise winning strategies for new or expanded business units. If the answer is to grow by capturing organic opportunities, you will want leaders who are good at nurturing internal talent.

For fast-growing high-tech companies, responding to changing context is critical. As the context changes, the behaviours leaders need to be successful also change. And that is why leadership development is a continuous journey.

3: Leadership is about what you do and say

There's no shortage of theories about leadership. If you do a search on Amazon, you'll find over 160,000 books on the subject. That would be a very long leadership development programme if you were to try and include all that they contain.

But leadership is not just about what people know. It's not just about what they think. It's mostly about what they do and say.

Think about the leaders you admire. What is it that you admire about them? If you're thinking about someone you've worked with, are you thinking about a conversation you had with them? Maybe you're thinking about how they reacted to bad news or dealt with a crisis. Maybe you're thinking about the vision they shared and how they wanted you to be part of it. Maybe you're thinking about some advice or ideas they gave you.

If you're thinking about someone famous, are you thinking about a speech you heard them make? Maybe you have a favourite quote of theirs, maybe a particular achievement that they were responsible for.

It doesn't matter which leader you're thinking of. What you admire about them is their behaviour, their actions. Nelson Mandela didn't just think abolishing apartheid was important, he took the action necessary to make it happen. Elon Musk isn't just knowledgeable about business and technology, he used that knowledge to co-found PayPal and put Tesla Motors on a world stage. Richard Branson has set up over 200 companies in more than thirty countries.

Underneath all this might be plenty of knowledge and critical thinking. But that alone isn't leadership. Leadership is behaviour, action – what you do and say. Leadership is influence – how what you do and say inspires others to act. And leadership is impact – how the actions of those you influence make a difference.

4: Leadership development needs behaviour change

Since leadership is behaviour, developing leadership within your company means changing people's behaviour.

People's behaviour is largely the result of their personality and character. It's driven by their beliefs and values. And they will have a myriad of automated responses which they have formed over many years.

So how do you change (ineffective) leadership behaviour? And, in a fast-moving organisation, how do you do it quickly?

The good news is that change – even radical change – is possible. And while it may not be overnight, there are ways to make the change happen quickly and sustainably.

The other good news is that changing behaviour is natural. From an early age, human beings become aware of new behaviours. Maybe their parents or teachers teach them, or they copy another child or sibling. And if the new behaviour works out well for them (it's fun; Mum's pleased with them; they get sweets) they'll try the behaviour again and again, until it becomes a natural part of their repertoire.

Learning new behaviours is no different for a leader in an organisation. It may be a bit more sophisticated, but it's no more complex.

5: You can't develop others

One of the most frequent questions I get asked by new managers is, 'How can I get people to do what I want them to do?' And the sad fact is you can't.

People have to develop themselves. And there lies the

challenge of leadership development. It's like all personal development that involves behaviour change. You can't stop smoking for someone. You can't do the workout for them. And you can't develop their career for them. All you can do is help them work out what they need to do and guide and support them as they take action.

The idea that managers and organisations can develop employees' careers is outdated. It may have been true once upon a time that employees would follow a predictable career path, but predictable career paths rely on static organisations. And in the fast-changing, high-growth tech sector, organisations aren't static. They are continually changing.

In today's world, career development is more like orienteering. The employee needs to take the lead on deciding where they want to go and how they're going to get there.

Reflect on your own career. Could you have predicted you would be where you are now? Did you follow a predictable path? Did you climb a ladder one step at a time? Or did you follow your own route?

Talented employees are happy to take responsibility for their professional development and career. But there is a high risk of losing them if they feel unsupported by their organisation. Effective leadership development needs a partnership between leaders and the organisation. High-tech companies need to empower employees to take ownership of their careers, making sure leadership development takes into account leaders' career ambitions. And both partners need to engage in career conversations so a connection can be made between the two.

LEADER – The proven six-step system

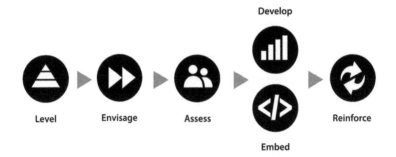

1. Level. What level are you currently at when it comes to developing leaders? What level do you need to be at? Build the business case for leadership development in your organisation.

2. Envisage the leaders you need for the future. Align leadership development with the business strategy and define the key metrics.

3. Assess the readiness of your potential leaders to take on new roles and responsibilities. How ready, willing and able are they?

4. Develop the skills, behaviours and confidence of your future leaders.

5. Embed. In parallel with Develop, embed new behaviours in the workplace to improve leadership on a day-to-day basis.

6. Reinforce and support new leadership behaviours through organisational routines, processes and systems.

Leadership development isn't 'just about running a training programme'. You need to take a strategic view, determining the leadership capacity, capability and culture required for success.

Fast-growing high-tech companies are busy. They are so busy focusing on the here and now that it's a challenge for them to concentrate on future growth. But leadership isn't about the here and now. Leadership is about the future. And the company needs leaders who can take them there.

Summary

This chapter has shown why leadership development is critical for fast, sustainable growth of your business, introducing the three biggest leadership challenges facing fast-growing high-tech organisations and how to identify which apply to your own company. It has covered the five guiding principles to follow when developing your leaders and an overview of the LEADER system to explain what each component is designed to achieve.

 The most important factor in getting results from this book is to take action. Spend a couple of minutes now thinking about the following questions:

❯ What are the key leadership challenges you currently face in your organisation?

❯ What would be the benefits of developing leaders in your organisation?

❯ What are the key questions you're hoping the book will answer?

The likelihood is, after reading this book you'll have a better understanding of what you want to achieve by developing your leaders, so you can come back and revisit these questions as you go through the book. But write your first thoughts now to get you started.

Chapter Two

Level

Building the business case

> *Effective leadership is not about making speeches or being liked; leadership is defined by results, not attributes.*

> PETER F. DRUCKER

How big a challenge is developing your leaders going to be? What level are you currently at when it comes to developing leaders? What level do you need to be at to be confident of developing the leaders you need for the future?

Whether you're a CEO or an HR professional, you can't do this alone. How are you going to get the buy-in and commitment of the senior executives and managers?

This chapter will help you address the following questions:

- Why do you need to take a long-term view when you have so many immediate challenges to focus on?
- What commitment do you need from others?
- What data will persuade key decision-makers to invest in leadership development?
- What is most important to key stakeholders?
- How will leadership development help their personal agenda?

Persuading others

Leadership development is something that every organisation knows it *should* do. But why? What will it help you achieve? What problems will it help you avoid or address? What would be the benefits of investing the time and money necessary for leadership development? If you don't have the answers, it will be hard to get the buy-in of the senior people who will need to support it.

Looking around the organisation, you might find it hard to see any need or urgency. Maybe you see that everyone is working hard, the business is doing well and you're not losing too many staff. Why worry about developing leaders when there's so much else to do?

But what if I told you there might be trouble lurking beneath the surface? That not taking steps now might result in massive issues in the not too distant future? The *Titanic* left it too late to steer away from the iceberg, most of which it couldn't see.

Leadership effectiveness is important. In fact, research[1] shows it is a more important measure of success than earnings forecast and ratio analysis. In its findings, Deloitte shares the following quotes from analysts:

> *I don't view financial performance as that important because I think it is only a result. Take Amazon as an example. Although it was in the red for years, real investors focused on the long-term potential value. I think all good performance is from good leadership.*
>
> ANALYST, CHINA

> *If the company has effective leadership it becomes a target for us. If not, we do not invest.*
>
> ASSET MANAGER, BRAZIL.

> *We look at the management qualities [of the company] and the track record of the people who are leading it and what they have done in the past. I would say [they can] add another 25–30% to the value of the company.*
>
> ANALYST, UNITED KINGDOM

> *I look at factors that go beyond specific financial factors. I can look at Return on Equity (ROE) and I can look at financial ratios as much as I want. But when you're looking at reputation you generally look on a broader scale. So I look*

---

1 Deloitte (2012), 'The Leadership Premium. How companies win the confidence of investors'

at media presence around the company, what people are saying, governance. I look for leadership factors in the CEO and the top leadership management.

MARKET ANALYST, UNITED STATES

Not developing your leaders might be fine if you want to stay small. If not, it will stunt your growth.

There is a clear connection between the quality of an organisation's leadership and employees' plans. Leadership influences whether employees stay with an organisation, perform well, and apply discretionary effort.

WHY LEADERSHIP DEVELOPMENT IS IMPORTANT

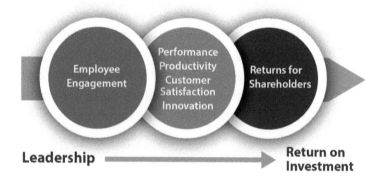

Better leadership can improve an organisation's bottom line by hundreds of thousands – or even millions – of dollars. The actual amount will depend on the size of the organisation and current gaps in leadership.

Putting off leadership development has a cost. You can manage successfully in the short-term, but it takes its toll long-term. To avoid your company ending up in a crisis, you need to take a step back and reflect on where you are with a few key measures.

Gather the data you need

Many business leaders struggle to appreciate that leadership development can add business value. But they do want better business results.

The business case needs to appeal both rationally and emotionally. You want your key stakeholders to wake up every morning committed to developing the company's leaders. That means you need to gather some key data and evidence.

The Economic Intelligence Unit[2] asked 300 business leaders, 'What business results would justify a large business investment?'

In response, 55% of business leaders said increased productivity, 40% wanted to see greater responsiveness to change (in other words, a more agile workforce), and 39% were looking for increased employee engagement. This focus is probably not a surprise because of the impact on customer satisfaction and revenue.

Leadership development has a direct impact on these.

---

2   Economic Intelligence Unit (2014), 'The C-Suite Imperative'.

THE VALUE OF LEADERSHIP DEVELOPMENT

Talent Development

9% reduction in attrition
17% improvement in engagement
14% improvement in productivity
12% reduction in time to competency

New Products/Services

Delivering new products and
services 23% faster
Rolling out new IT applications
26% faster

Gaining Market Share

17% rise in customer satisfaction
10% improvement in revenue

Delivering Efficiency

17% Cost Reduction
21% increase in volume
22% reduction in delivery time
20% reduction in study time

Bottom-line impact of learning innovation over three years (2014 Towards Maturity Benchmark)

The data you gather will depend on the specifics of your business. Typically, leadership effectiveness divides into two categories – leadership activities (inputs) and leadership impact (outputs).

Examples of inputs include:

People development. How much money have you spent on leadership training and development?

People review. How much time has the leadership team spent discussing leadership issues/opportunities? Is it part of a regular meeting agenda? What actions have you decided? What actions have you taken?

People performance. How many performance discussions have taken place? What is the distribution of performance ratings?

People objectives. How many goal setting discussions have taken place? What objectives have been set?

Examples of outputs include:

People turnover. How many people have left (or are due to leave) as a % of total headcount? What is the trend?

People absence. How many days' sickness and how many instances of sickness per employee are there annually? What is the trend?

People engagement. What is the overall satisfaction? (Undertake an engagement survey to answer this.) What is the trend?

People growth. What is the increase in headcount? What is the trend?

People progression. How many people have you progressed or promoted into new roles?

Business impact – data around revenue, productivity, customer satisfaction.

I recommend you gather the data into a dashboard that you can then use for reporting purposes. What does it tell you? What business problems can you infer from the data?

Specific questions to answer are:

> ❯ How productive are your people?
>
> ❯ How engaged are your people?
>
> ❯ What is retention like?
>
> ❯ Are you keeping your best people?
>
> ❯ How many leaders do you have at each level?
>
> ❯ What are the plans for headcount growth?
>
> ❯ How many vacancies for leaders do you have?

> How much time are you spending on developing your leaders?

> How much money are you spending on developing your leaders?

> Who sponsors leadership development?

Quantitative data (statistics, surveys, benchmarks) is valuable, but it's just one part of the picture. I recommend you also gather qualitative data (feedback, testimonials, case studies). This will allow you to address the business impact while making an emotional connection.

I had an interesting experience of the different pictures that come from data vs people when I started working with a fast-growing consultancy company. It dominated the market in its specialist area and had been hugely successful, growing by over 40% year on year. This growth had relied on the company recruiting trainee consultants at the bottom of the organisational hierarchy so new employees could do the job as soon as they'd completed their induction.

As the company grew, it rewarded successful performance with promotion and some staff had risen quickly through the ranks. But the downside was that people in management positions had no previous leadership experience. It was a classic case of *The Peter Principle*.

The Peter Principle is a book written in 1968 by L. J. Peter. In it he states:

In a hierarchy every employee tends to rise to his level of incompetence...in time every post tends to be occupied by an employee who is incompetent to carry out its duties... Work is accomplished by those employees who have not yet reached their level of incompetence.

That was the case with my client company, and it recognised this had created difficulties. Its data showed that 50% of new recruits left the company within their first six months, and it had lots of plausible explanations for this data which included: 'Our reputation for training is so good that employees get approached by our competitors who can afford to offer higher salaries because they don't have to train them' and 'Millennials are fickle. They've no staying power'.

The picture I got when I talked to people within the organisation gave a different point of view. It was a picture of a bullying, autocratic culture. Managers tried to get their people to do what they wanted by shouting at and belittling them. Every employee described excessive hours and lack of opportunity to take breaks or holiday entitlements. They talked of difficulty in managing their wellbeing.

That is not a sustainable culture for employees. It was not a surprise that turnover was high.

I believe both views were accurate. But it shows you need both the data and the stories to understand what's happening.

What is most important to key stakeholders?

Business people like to think they make decisions based on logic and rationale. But they're human too. People make decisions based on emotion. They then reconcile and justify those decisions with data and evidence.

The data will be the same for every person you talk to. But the meaning of that data will differ according to what's important to them. For example, a high attrition rate will concern everyone but for different reasons. The Finance Director will be concerned about the high costs of replacing and recruiting. The HR Director will share that concern, but will also be frustrated that the HR team is swamped with recruitment requests. Meanwhile, the Operations Director will panic about client service.

People will be motivated if you appeal to their self-interest. But even more powerful is describing what people stand to lose if nothing changes. Various experiments have shown that the risk of losing something they already have – whether it's time, money, the competitive advantage, their reputation – is more likely to motivate people to act than the idea of gaining that same thing. So, when you're putting together your business case, think about what whomever you'll be presenting it to might lose if the organisation doesn't invest in leadership development.

That is what I had to do with the fast-growing consultancy I mentioned earlier. No development programme was in place to help newly promoted managers, and the most senior leaders lacked coaching and mentoring skills. Lack of leadership throughout the organisation was the biggest challenge it faced, and the biggest concern for investors. But it was still a challenge to persuade leaders that they needed to invest time and money in developing their leadership skills rather than just focusing on delivery.

After spending some time with the leaders, I learned that they were proud of three things – entrepreneurial growth, brand reputation and personal success (financial and professional). All these things were at risk if they didn't develop themselves and others.

Work out the benefits or losses to each stakeholder of agreeing or not agreeing to invest in leadership development.

And make sure your business case appeals to each one individually.

Here are some suggested questions to explore with each stakeholder:

❯ What is your understanding of the overall vision, mission and strategies for the company?

❯ What is the role of your division of the business in helping to achieve the company's vision, mission and strategies?

❯ What is driving the focus for this financial year?

❯ What does success look like for your division? What are its specific goals, objectives and measures?

❯ Where is the division starting from? What are the current strengths and issues with performance?

❯ What will be the main challenges for the division in achieving the goals and objectives?

❯ What attitudes, skills and knowledge will employees need to address the challenges and achieve the goals and objectives?

❯ What do you sense to be the key gaps in attitudes, skills and behaviours?

❯ What key priorities in development areas do you need to address?

❯ What will help or hinder the division in addressing these development areas (time, resources, attitudes of employees, attitudes of managers, etc.)?

❯ What can you do to take advantage of the supporting factors and minimise the barriers?

Summary

This chapter focused on your starting point, recommending you start with a Level activity to understand the size of the challenge you are facing. How are you going to get the buy-in of the senior executives you need to help you?

It's important to take a long-term view even when you have many immediate challenges to focus on, and for this you need commitment from others. Data can persuade key decision makers to invest time and money in leadership development, but it's also important to find out what matters most to key stakeholders so you can decide how leadership development can help them.

Complete a fact-finding exercise. Gather data about talent development and quantify the problem you need to address.

Hold discussions with key stakeholders. Understand their drivers and what is important to them.

Put together a compelling business case. Gain commitment and agreement to investing in leadership development.

Chapter Three

Envisage
Adopting a strategic approach to developing leaders

If you're not sure where you are going, you're liable to end up someplace else.

ROBERT F. MAGER

Did you know that only a quarter of organisations say their leadership development programmes are effective at improving performance? Research by McKinsey[1] shows that one of the biggest mistakes companies make is they don't align their leadership development strategy with their business strategy.

---

1   McKinsey (2014), 'Why Leadership Development Programs Fail'

The Envisage component involves analysing the organisation strategy and the leadership roles, skills and behaviours that you need to deliver it.

In this chapter we'll look at the importance of business strategy to leadership development planning, gaining a clear vision of leadership for your high-tech organisation. How can you identify the leadership roles, skills and behaviours that will be critical to growth?

Leadership that is fit for purpose

I've had a couple of clients ask me for examples of 'world-class' leadership development, mentoring programmes or coaching programmes. To be honest, the questions make me nervous.

Now don't get me wrong, I am all for learning from the experiences of others. Hearing what other companies have done can stimulate great ideas and creativity. But you're doomed if you slavishly copy the approach of another organisation.

In my humble opinion, world-class leadership development is characterised by one overriding principle: it is designed specifically to meet the needs of one organisation and its employees, developing leaders who can deliver strategy and drive business results.

When I left P&G, I moved to the head office of Prontaprint, a print franchise organisation. I had ambitious, large-scale ideas based on my experience of P&G and what, no doubt, would be considered world-class training and development. My ideas included introducing a performance management process, coaching and mentoring initiatives and training programmes for managers and leaders.

But, ambitious ideas weren't what the company needed then. The world was changing to one where every company had their own in-house printer, so Prontaprint leaders had to change too. They were used to a retail focus where customers walked through the door. Instead, they had to adopt a sales focus and promote their services to other businesses. From a leadership development perspective, the critical individuals were the MDs of each business, and the immediate priority was for Prontaprint to develop its sales and marketing skills to make that transformation. My ideas on introducing people management practices were good, but they were based on what I thought was important, not on what the company needed.

Companies that consistently produce great talent and grow successfully do not have the most sophisticated or complex leadership development practices. Instead they have practices that are fit for purpose, suit their culture, are relatively simple and are executed flawlessly.

World-class leadership development is designed to drive business results. No more, no less.

The importance of business strategy

Leadership is about the future. Fast-growing high-tech companies need leaders who can take them there. So, what better way to develop your future leaders than by engaging them *now* in creating the business they will be running?

Too often companies define the leadership development strategy as being separate and independent of the business strategy. That is not just poor practice, it's plain wrong.

Your business goals drive the quality and quantity of leaders you need. And your strategy will be unique to the business context you are working in. As a fast-growing company, you will need to focus on bringing in new people, expanding rapidly and building your employment brand. Depending on your growth plans, you might need to increase the number of leaders at every level by 10% or more every year over the next three years.

If you're at a stage of globalising the business, your focus might be on integrating recruitment with an internal mobility programme. If you're suffering from low engagement and employee performance, your focus might be on revamping performance discussions and development.

A technology company recently came to me after internal discussions around their lack of a leadership pipeline. It was a specialised IT company that had grown rapidly over the past five years and was finding it hard to recruit from outside. Its attrition was not too bad even though it was a tough environment, but the senior staff knew their people were young, hungry and ambitious. They wanted to make sure they looked after them, kept them and developed them.

Their number one question was, 'How do we define talent?'

The reality is that there is no single definition of talent or leadership. It will depend on what you're trying to achieve as a business.

When you're developing leaders, the starting point is to be clear on what kind of business you need to be in the future. Wherever your focus, you need to answer these questions:

- ❷ What is the organisation vision and business strategy that our leaders need to deliver?
- ❷ What are the key roles to help us overcome our business challenges?

❯ What leadership skills do we need to realise our vision?

❯ What culture do we need to develop leadership throughout the organisation?

Develop a clear vision of leadership

The first step in defining your leadership strategy is to review the vision and strategy for the organisation. Identify the key drivers that will be critical for the organisation's success, i.e. the relatively few (three to five) determinants of sustainable competitive advantage for your company in your industry.

Drivers are the choices that leaders make about how to position the organisation. That position should take advantage of its strengths and weaknesses as an organisation, recognising the opportunities and threats in the marketplace. Drivers make a strategy unique to one organisation compared to another, dictate where trade-offs can be made between resources, time and energy, and help you understand what it is essential for leaders of the organisation to do.

You can identify the key drivers by asking a few fundamental questions:

❯ Is this driver an organisational talent that is absolutely vital?

❯ Could something else be more essential in making the vision and mission happen?

❯ Defined relatively, what is most important to our success and our ability to compete?

❯ Is this something the organisation is positioned to do better than its competitors?

❯ Will doing this well translate directly into continued or future success?

❯ Would not doing this well cause the organisation to fail?

For example, if the business strategy is 'becoming more global', the implications for leaders would be:

❯ Need for greater cultural sensitivity

❯ Increased representation of different geographies at top levels

❯ Improved language skills in key leadership roles to enable cross-cultural relationship building

❯ Heightened importance of foreign assignments for future leaders

❯ Greater understanding of local laws and business arrangements in strategy making.

If the primary focus is 'becoming more innovative', the implications for leaders would be:

❯ Greater collaboration to bring new products to market

❯ Increased involvement in gathering consumer insights and translating these into profitable ideas for new products

❯ Anticipating capital, space, talent implications of a rapidly expanding product portfolio

❯ Cultural change to create a spirit of innovation versus a culture of risk aversion at top levels of the organisation.

The key drivers and their associated business strategies will have clear implications: they state what leaders must do well for the organisation to succeed. That will allow you to define the skills and behaviours your leaders will need to be successful.

How to identify the critical leadership roles

While every role in your company is important, not every role is critical or strategic. Critical roles will vary by company, and aren't always high profile. A little digging will reveal them in your company.

Consider a coffee-shop chain. You might assume the leadership roles with the biggest influence on performance would be those responsible for recruiting, managing and developing the baristas. And you'd be partly right if a key part of the business proposition is customer service. But if the company proposition is more focused on price than service, the leaders of the buyers who negotiate coffee bean prices will play an equally important role.

In P&G, for example, the business proposition is heavily focused on product performance. One of the key differentiators for a new product is its perfume. You might wonder why fragrance is such a big deal, but human psychology is a funny thing. The perfume of a detergent doesn't just influence whether a consumer likes the smell, it affects their perception of how well the product cleans and softens the clothes. Two identical formulations with different perfumes can perform significantly differently in consumer tests. In the highly competitive detergent industry, the Head of Perfumery role is a critical one.

There are three kinds of roles that exist within every company.

Organisational leadership roles

Organisational leadership roles are concerned with the future, with big decisions, the shape and scope of the business and the culture.

About 10–15% of roles within an organisation are strategic. Obvious roles are the CEO, the Chief Financial Officer or the Chief Technology Officer of the company. There may also be less obvious strategic roles within your organisation. Explore your business proposition and you might just find some surprises.

Functional leadership roles

Functional leadership roles are concerned with optimising core processes. They may be your manufacturing roles if you are manufacturing technology products. They may be software developer roles if you sell an online solution. They may be your project management roles if you are a consultancy selling solutions.

These roles are vital to the organisation, yet their importance is often secondary to the more organisational leadership roles. Functional leadership roles make up around 60% of all leadership roles.

People leadership roles

People leadership roles make up 20–25% of the organisation and are concerned with making it work better. Again, these roles are vitally important to the success of the organisation, but they are not strategic.

These levels of leadership are not synonymous with business function. A single function (Finance, HR, Sales, etc.) will likely have a mixture of all three levels.

Understanding these roles in any organisation is central to building a leadership development model. You recognise immediately where you need to put your energy. You are clear on where you need your best people. You know which roles are most important for the organisation. And you can assess whether the people you have in those roles are the best people for the organisation.

Here are five important questions to ask to identify the pivotal roles in your company:

1. **Where does it matter most for the organisation to have better quality leaders?** As much as you may want 'A players' in every position, that's simply not realistic. Not every role needs an A player, nor can every company afford to pay for one for every role. Identify which roles really need to have the highest quality talent.

2. **Where is the organisation most constrained by a lack of leaders?** Sometimes the issue may not be that your organisation needs leaders with better or different skills. It may have processes in place that work well to develop skills. But organisations are sometimes challenged to identify the feeder pool. Or they may struggle to find enough leaders to fill pivotal positions.

3. **What specific business drivers or strategies does a pivotal role impact?** Identify what makes a role pivotal. What strategies or competitive differentiators are at risk if the company doesn't have enough of these leaders? What if these leaders do not perform at a high enough level?

4. **How or why is one leadership role more pivotal than others?** Sometimes, even for roles at the same level, some positions are more pivotal. For example, if the company's growth strategy involves expanding into

specific countries, the managers of those countries may be more pivotal than other countries' managers.

5. **What is the expected turnover rate and headcount growth needed for pivotal roles?** It's important to know the anticipated talent flow through pivotal roles for workforce planning. Do people become frustrated with their roles and often leave? Are they easily recruited by competitors, or do they stay in their roles for years?

Answering these questions can help you decide the extent and urgency of business risk. Then you can decide whether to build or buy the talent you need.

Define leadership skills and behaviours

The next step is to define the leadership skills and *behaviours* you need to realise your vision. I emphasise behaviours because you need to focus on observable actions that will deliver business results.

For example, in the early years of Avanade, a key driver was our partnership with our parent companies, Accenture and Microsoft. Our strategy was to collaborate to achieve agreed goals around revenue and market share. To be successful required leadership skills and behaviours that were defined as:

> *The Avanade leader must be continuously conscious of our partnerships, building relationships with Microsoft and Accenture on a number of levels. They should know when and how to engage partners for mutual success and how to manage any conflicts. In public,*

they should strive to project Avanade's team-work-driven role in these relationships.

Defining the desired leadership skills and behaviours is a creative process which can be challenging for even the most strategic of thinkers.

There are a variety of methods that can help. One way is to use a tool called the 'Future Perfect', drawn from an approach called 'Solutions Focus'.[2]

'Future Perfect' involves projecting oneself into a future when the organisation is fully implementing its strategy and delivering results. Key stakeholders are asked to describe what the leadership culture looks like in that future. What behaviours are they observing? What are the signs and indicators that there is a strong leadership culture within the organisation? What positive comments are employees, customers and other stakeholders making about leadership in general? What processes are in place to reinforce the positive leadership behaviours? What behaviours are called out as indicative of good leadership and rewarded accordingly?

It may sound a bit crazy as an approach because it is not typical of the discussions we have in business. But believe me, it works well. It is unfailing in its ability to energise key stakeholders and gain their commitment to a shared picture of success.

I cannot emphasise this enough: it's really important to develop a definition of leadership that is specific to your organisation and your strategy. It always amazes me when

---

2   Paul Z. Jackson, Mark McKergow (2007), *The Solutions Focus: Making Coaching and Change SIMPLE.*

companies ask for an off-the-shelf leadership framework. Since leaders are key competitive advantages, why would anyone want to develop them to be exactly the same as everyone else's leaders?

But I do understand the challenge of defining leadership starting with a blank sheet of paper. Sometimes it can be helpful to start with a generic set of leadership skills and behaviours, then you select the ones that will be most important for delivering your strategy, rephrasing them so they sound like your company. Don't talk about 'show initiative' if the words your leaders use are 'step up to the mark'.

So where can you find a generic set of leadership capabilities that contribute to the success of high-growth companies? One source of such knowledge is India.

Key leadership capabilities

In India, many home-grown businesses are seeking to double, triple and quadruple their revenues over the next decade, if not sooner. Companies have begun to show great interest in investing in leadership development.

So what can we learn from their experience? How does it apply to us in the Western world?

In 2008 the Tata Management Training Center (TMTC) and the Center for Creative Leadership (CCL-Asia) published a report called 'Developing Future Leaders for High-Growth Indian Companies'.[3] This report summarised their research with seventy-one executives from eight high-growth global Indian companies, detailing four general areas of capability:

3   Center for Creative Leadership and Tata Management Training Center (2008), 'Developing Future Leaders for High-Growth Indian Companies'.

Leading self: skills and behaviours related to the inner world of leaders and effective ways to manage themselves – their thoughts, emotions, actions, and attitudes – over time. Specific lessons include confidence; self-awareness; understanding and committing to life goals; and integrity – i.e., the essentials of self-management.

Leading others: behaviours related to the interpersonal and social skills that equip leaders to connect with and influence people. Specific lessons include managing and motivating subordinates; developing subordinates; and team management/development – i.e., the essentials of relationship management.

Leading the business: skills and behaviours related to the world of running a business and facilitating the accomplishment of work in organisations. Specific lessons include execution and operational management; innovation, creativity, and entrepreneurship; functional knowledge; and gathering information, knowledge, and insight – i.e., the essentials of managing a unit, department, or the organisation.

Meaning of leadership: skills and behaviours related to reflecting on experience. These lessons are distilled from years of experience, resulting in a leader's personal formula for successfully leading self, others, and the business.

Are the leadership capabilities any different from those we would expect in a high growth organisation? Probably not. Can you pick them up and use them for your organisation? Definitely not. But they provide a helpful framework, serving as a starting point for identifying the leadership capabilities for your own business strategy.

THE MEANING OF LEADERSHIP

Leading Self	Leading Others	Leading the Business
Fix Confidence*	Managing and Motivating Subordinates*	Execution & Operating Savvy*
Self-Awareness*	Developing Subordinates*	Innovation, Creativity & Entrepreneurship*
Understanding & Committing to Life Goals*	Team Management*	Functional Knowledge*
Integrity*	Cultural Savvy	Gathering Information, Knowledge & Insights*
Becoming Humane	Building Relationships with Peers and Seniors	Decision-making & Problem-solving
Dealing with Setbacks	Building Credibility	Acquiring a Broad Organisational View & Strategic Insight
Developing Flexibility & Adaptability	Communication & Feedback	Customer Orientation
Seeing Things From a New Perspective	Gaining Influence	Handling Organizational & Cultural Change
Dealing with Ambiguity	Managing Multiple Stakeholders	

*Top 11 lessons - Source: Developing Future Leaders for High-Growth Indian Companies: New Perspectives (Center for Creative Leadership & TATA)

How to envisage leadership

The following is the process I use with my clients to carry out the Envisage component of the LEADER system. First, schedule time with the leadership or management team you are working with. I recommend a minimum of half a day, preferably away from the office, as strategic thinking is always done best off site.

A sample agenda is as follows:

Step 1	*Organisation strategy*	Review the organisation vision and strategy
Step 2	*'Future Perfect' Activity*	The more visual you make the activity, the better. I often encourage clients to come up with posters or storyboards so that we focus on behaviours that people can observe rather than concepts and ideas that they can't.
Step 3	*Leadership behaviours*	Provide a list of leadership behaviours and ask each team member to select a minimum of three and a maximum of five that they believe will be needed to deliver the organisation vision and strategy. To help your thought process, below is a list of real-world leadership behaviours. This will generate a long list so that you can see all the possibilities. Your company's leadership behaviours are somewhere in that long list.
Step 4	*Shortlisting*	Narrow it down. In your first edit, circle which ones are truly important. Draw a line through those that are not. Combine those that are similar. After the first round, you should have the list down to somewhere between five and fifteen.
Step 5	*Prioritising*	Here is where you're going to have to make some tough decisions. Decide which behaviours will really make a difference to the business. The rule of thumb is to reach a final list of between five and seven.
Step 6	*Describing*	When writing your leadership behaviours, make sure you word each behaviour with a verb describing the *action* expected. And make sure you give a supporting example. Below is an example of a Leader Profile.

Leadership behaviours

Business	*Business acumen*	Possesses basic knowledge of business processes and procedures
	Strategic vision	Recognises long-term business opportunities and implications
	Decision making	Evaluates potential courses of action from a range of alternatives
	Continuous learning	Takes advantage of opportunities to learn and stay current
	Problem solving	Identifies a workable solution from a range of alternatives
	Tactical reasoning	Evaluates the risks and opportunities in day-to-day business transactions
People	*Employee development*	Improves the ability of team members to beat the competition
	Building teams	Acquires and develops the talent necessary to beat the competition
	Delegation	Gets work done through others
	Initiative	Takes action without being told to do so
	Managing performance	Provides feedback about the accomplishment of objectives
	Resource management	Allocates time, people and equipment to beat the competition

Interpersonal	*Trustworthiness*	Secures the confidence of others through consistent words and actions
	Building relationships	Establishes and maintains positive rapport with others
	Influencing others	Utilises the power of persuasion to gain the support of others
	Service orientation	Responds to others on time to meet their needs
	Teamwork	Works co-operatively with others to accomplish goals or objectives
	Interpersonal communication	Interacts effectively with others to convey thoughts and ideas
Intrapersonal	*Dependability*	Reliably follows through on commitments made to others
	Flexibility	Willing to take alternative actions given appropriate justification
	Stress tolerance	Maintains stable performance under the pressures of work or life
	Planning	Looks forward in addressing tasks to anticipate steps and contingences
	Detail orientation	Attends to all steps and follow-ups necessary to do a task
	Professionalism	Conducts oneself with high standards and integrity

Example Leader Profile

To be a leader at Geek Inc. is to be accountable for consistently delivering business results. To excel requires that you master the following set of skills and activities:

1. To generate a high win/loss ratio and deliver large, impactful deals optimised for success, leaders must build lasting business relationships.

   > *"The Geek leader connects quickly with customers and builds deep relationships by empathising with the customer's pain and being able to converse in the language of their business. The leader can paint a picture of their world and establish clear expectations of the better future Geek Inc. can deliver."*

2. To manage risk, our leaders must effectively estimate, plan, and deliver projects and maximise customer satisfaction.

   > *"Our leaders must be willing to operate at a level of detail that gives the customer and our project teams confidence. A leader must be fully aware of the strengths and weaknesses of any plan, proposal, or deal we put in front of a customer."*

3. To ensure our market position as a leading provider of technological solutions, our leaders need to inspire, energise, and empower their teams.

   > *"The Geek leader sets a clear vision for the team and supports the establishment and attainment of personal goals. He leads with a consistent and predictable style. He communicates regularly and motivates the team through recognition, rewards, and celebration of success. His actions inspire confidence and creativity."*

5. To ensure ongoing technical competency, our leaders must demonstrate a passion for technology.

   "We expect our leaders to stay current on the latest trends both with established and developing technologies."

6. To grow the organisation and build capability to execute against project challenges, leaders must effectively recruit talented people and develop leaders.

   "The Geek leader needs to be a role model for her team. She needs to create a culture of continuous learning while mentoring and developing the next generation of leaders. She should effectively delegate and offer challenges that will foster team growth. She should understand the financial impact of recruiting decisions and know when and who to hire."

Summary

In this chapter, we've looked at the importance of business strategy to leadership development, learning how to identify the leadership roles that will be critical to growth. We've discovered a way of developing a clear vision of leadership for an organisation and how to define the leadership skills and behaviours that will be necessary for business success.

Now it's time to put it all into practice. Gather the information available on the business strategy and schedule a leadership team meeting to carry out the following:

❯ Review the organisation strategy and complete the 'Future Perfect' activity

❯ Identify the roles that will be pivotal to success

❯ Define the leadership skills and behaviours you need.

Chapter Four

Assess Part 1
Organisation and employee perspectives

> *The best way to predict your future is to create it.*
>
> **ABRAHAM LINCOLN**

Once you've defined what successful leadership means for your company, you'll want to assess your people. How ready, willing and able are your potential leaders to take on new roles and responsibilities?

When I was a single woman in my twenties, my friends and I took great pleasure in visiting a clairvoyant about once a year.

'We're not taking it seriously,' we said to each other. 'It's just a laugh.'

But, as insecure young women uncertain about our futures, we secretly hoped there was something in it. Would we make the progress we hoped for in our careers? Would we meet the man of our dreams? Would we travel the world? There was no scientific basis to the clairvoyant's reading and no guarantee that anything she said would come true, and yet we clung to anything that matched the future we hoped for, ignoring anything that didn't quite fit our dreams.

Like clairvoyance, leadership development is trying to anticipate the future. And unfortunately, in many companies the approach is no more scientific.

The Assess component of the LEADER system takes the guesswork out of your planning.

In this chapter, we'll look at two perspectives – the organisation's and the employee's. We'll learn how to take a more scientific and objective approach to identifying leaders with the potential to grow the company, understanding the difference between performance and potential and learning how to assess technical employees for leadership potential. This will help to develop a robust people plan for a growing organisation.

Organisation and employee

When appointing any new leader, we want to look for someone who will perform a role to deliver the vision and goals of the organisation. There are three questions we need to ask about each individual:

❯ Is the individual **ready** to commit to the organisation, its vision and values?

❯ Is the individual **willing** to take on the challenges and responsibilities involved in the new role?

❯ Is the individual **able**? Do they have the skills and behaviours needed to perform their new responsibilities successfully?

An employee's performance in a broader role is influenced by three things:

Ability – are they confident they have the skills and experience to perform in their new role?

Motivation – do they want the changes that come with the new role, for example, prestige and recognition? Advancement and influence? Work-life balance? Job enjoyment?

Opportunity – do they feel the organisation will provide them with the career opportunities they are looking for? Do they think they will have the resources to carry out the role to the level needed?

TWO PERSPECTIVES TO CONSIDER

As pictured above, there is a need to create alignment between the ambitions of the organisation and the ambitions of the individual. Wherever possible, give people the opportunity and ability to do what they have the potential and motivation to do.

Effective leadership development relies on evolving roles as well as developing individuals, so adjust the roles in the organisation to fit the strengths of the people available. At the same time, develop (and recruit) leaders to meet the needs of the organisation.

Leadership development needs a partnership approach, creating a fit between the ambitions of your organisation and its potential leaders.

Identifying leaders with potential

One of the key challenges with assessing leaders is the concept of 'potential'. What is 'high potential'? High potential for what?

Potential is the difference between an individual's current performance and their greatest performance – in other words, what they could achieve given every opportunity and no constraints.

Think about future leaders in the context of the future. What does the organisation need to realise its vision and deliver the strategy?

Some companies I know have adapted this idea to mean those individuals who have 'what it takes' to get to the top – or at least close to the top. Naturally, this is hard to measure or predict. Two managers might be equally effective in their current role, but one might have a far greater positive impact as a member of the Board. It's important to remember that the leadership needs of the organisation will change over time. So leaders and potential leaders will need to evolve and develop in line with those changes.

One of the companies I worked with defined a person's potential as 'the ability to be promoted two levels above where they are'. I asked the Head of HR how we could identify those people. His response?

'They just have that extra something. I know it when I see it.'

That is deeply unhelpful and fatally flawed. Without an objective description, there is no benchmark to evaluate different individuals. And there is no model for employees to work towards.

To develop leaders, you need an approach that you can communicate and apply consistently.

When we talk about potential, what we really mean is **someone who is ready, willing and able to rise to and succeed in a challenging role that is critical to the success of the organisation.**

In other words, based on what we know now, do we think an individual could take on a leadership role? If not, what would they need to develop or change to be ready in the future?

This approach serves two purposes. Firstly, it recognises that change is happening all the time – especially in fast-growing companies. Any assessment is simply a snapshot at a moment in time. Secondly, it places the focus on development.

It may be that some people will never be ready, willing and able to take on a leadership role. But at least the door remains open to them if they know what the organisation is looking for.

What is the difference between performance and potential?

Did you know that only one in seven high performers actually has the potential to be successful in higher-level leadership roles? That's the conclusion of research by the Corporate Executive Board.[1] But sadly many organisations still assume that a high performer has the potential for a higher-level leadership role.

Past performance is a predictor of future performance, but only when the challenges and roles remain consistent. Significantly different challenges lie ahead in leadership roles, so it is critical to distinguish and test potential and readiness. Without the relevant support to develop their skills and confidence, there's a strong likelihood that people will struggle with the new leadership role. And that will be to the detriment of the company's growth and success.

Leadership potential is about having the capacity and motivation to quickly develop the qualities needed for success in a broader, more challenging and higher-level position.

performance *(noun)*
> an individual's level of success in executing objectives in their current (or past) roles. Includes demonstration of required competencies.

potential *(noun)*
> the likelihood that an individual can develop into a successful leader with significantly expanded, higher-level leadership responsibilities.

---

1   Corporate Executive Board (2005), 'Improving the Odds of Success for High-Potential Programmes'.

Research by the Corporate Executive Board shows there is a way to identify people with leadership potential.[2]

They are proven high performers with three distinguishing qualities which allow them to rise and succeed in higher-level leadership roles.

1. Aspiration – they are motivated and **willing** to take on more challenging, higher-level roles.

2. Ability – they are **able** to be effective in more responsible roles and display the skills and behaviours needed.

3. Engagement – they are **ready** to commit to the organisation and remain in challenging roles.

LEADERSHIP POTENTIAL

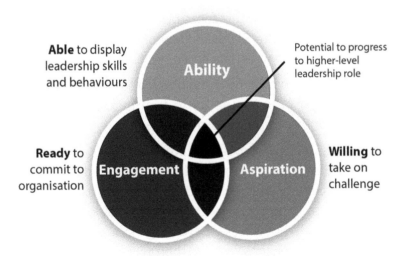

Able to display leadership skills and behaviours

Ability

Potential to progress to higher-level leadership role

Ready to commit to organisation

Engagement

Aspiration

Willing to take on challenge

---

2   Corporate Executive Board (2005), 'Realizing the Full Potential of Rising Talent: A Quantitative Analysis of the Identification and Development of High-potential'.

In essence, high-potential employees like what they do, want to do more and always go the extra mile. They see a future for themselves in your organisation.

These three qualities have proven to be robust in identifying people with true leadership potential – whether you're in banking in Hong Kong or software development in London.

Trying to predict how someone might perform in the future is always a gamble. By assessing the readiness, willingness and ability of your people, you make your odds of success much greater.

How to assess technical employees for leadership potential

The key challenge with assessing future leaders is that you need to be able to take a view of someone. And this has to be done in a serious and objective way.

Does the person have the ambition to reach a senior position? Do they have the ability to turn that ambition into success for them and the organisation?

People with leadership potential embody energy and enthusiasm for their roles, their organisation and their industry. They are often looking for stretching developmental experiences, constantly seeking their next challenge. They don't simply follow the status quo, instead showing leadership by inspiring and motivating those around them. Often, these kinds of behaviours become clear early on in an individual's career.

The onus is not just on managers to notice these types of traits, it's on everyone who has a vested interest in managing the talent within an organisation. And this is normally only the first stage.

Are your people ready to become leaders?

It's all very well that your people are high performers. But they have to be engaged and committed to your organisation. And a staggering 55% will leave you, so you need to check engagement.

Employee engagement is an idea that is widely accepted but loosely defined. An employee's commitment to your company depends on two factors:

1. Past and current experiences (positive or negative) with their job, role and work environment. Every day, their experiences, interactions with other staff and managers, their work challenges and the culture of the organisation can make or break your potential leaders' commitment.

2. Future expectations about their job, career and your company as an employer. How the future looks and feels to your people is important. They are going to be as interested in whether they agree with the organisation's vision and goals as they are in their own challenges and ambitions.

COMPONENTS OF EMPLOYEE ENGAGEMENT

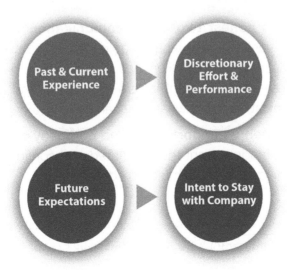

Potential high-tech leaders are in demand. Yes, you want them, but then so does everyone else – including your competitors. Is the organisation delivering on its implied promises? Be assured, it isn't all about the money (even though money is often the default excuse when a high potential individual leaves).

Research by Culture Amp[3] shows that the most important components for engaging high-tech employees are:

Company seen as a great place to develop. Potential high-tech leaders are more likely to commit to your organisation if they can see clear opportunities for development, experience and movement.

Confidence in the leaders. By their nature, fast-growing high-tech companies involve risk and uncertainty. To commit to the organisation, potential leaders need to think the company and their careers are in good hands.

Company effectively directs resources (funding, people and effort) towards company goals. Potential leaders are ambitious and driven. They want to know they will have access to the resources they need to do a good job.

Open and honest two-way communication. Potential leaders want to know what is going on in the company. They want more feedback on their performance. They want an honest assessment of where they stand and greater communication about what they can do to improve.

People seen as important to the company's success. Potential leaders want to feel valued and confident they will be given the opportunity to contribute.

---

3   Culture Amp (2016), 'New Tech – Benchmark Report'.

When evaluating if someone is ready to be a leader, answer the following questions:

- ❯ Is this individual proud to work for the organisation?
- ❯ Does this individual speak positively about the organisation?
- ❯ Does the organisation mean a lot to this individual?
- ❯ Does this individual believe the best way to advance in his or her career is to stay with the organisation?
- ❯ Does this individual often try to help others who have heavy workloads?

Suppose Mary has been with a company for two years. In a recent career conversation with her manager she revealed that she enjoys her work, but she also has ambitions. She said that she wants to apply for a role in a different part of the company: one that will challenge her and help her develop further.

As well as having the ambition to expand her skills and grow, she is clearly committed to the organisation. She's ready for new challenges in her career and sees opportunities to aim for them in the company. This is a great time to engage and develop Mary in a way that benefits her and the organisation.

Are your people willing to be leaders?

The big question is, 'Does Mary want to take on the responsibilities, challenges and rewards typically associated with more senior roles?' Not everyone does. Does she have the critical career management behaviours to succeed? Is she likely to rise to a senior and more challenging position and turn that motivation into career success?

Research has shown that people who have the aspiration to take on leadership roles are driven by the following six factors:

❯ **Immersion –** they look for roles that need a personal commitment above the norm

❯ **Activity –** they prefer fast-paced, multi-tasking work environments

❯ **Power –** they want the opportunity to influence and shape how things are done

❯ **Interest –** they look for roles and assignments that provide variety and stimulation

❯ **Flexibility –** they seek work environments that allow them more fluid ways of working

❯ **Autonomy –** they are attracted to roles that allow them autonomy in how they carry out their responsibilities.

It may be possible to assess Mary's drivers through career conversations with her, or by using carefully selected psychometric assessments that look at her work values. Does she use initiative and take responsibility? Is she willing to take calculated risks? Does she take on positions of responsibility so she can impact tasks, projects and objectives?

Does she push for results? Is she willing to invest in her personal development? Do others look to her for answers and input? Is she regularly invited to attend groups for her insight and ideas? In meetings, do people listen to her more than others?

When assessing whether Mary is willing to be a leader, her manager would strive to answer the following questions:

❯ Is it important to her to rise to a senior management position at this or another organisation?

❯ Is it important to her to receive at least one promotion in her career?

❯ Is it important to her to be recognised as an expert in her field by people in and outside of the organisation?

❯ Is it important to her to receive greater and greater amounts of responsibility over the course of her career?

❯ Is it important to her to receive increases in recognition and reward over the course of her career?

Are your people able to be leaders?

There are many things to look at when assessing Mary.

General demands. Does she gather information from all available sources before drawing conclusions? Can she logically piece together a solution to a problem? Does she absorb complex ideas and incorporate them into her work? Can she effectively manage difficult employees and inspire others? Does she remain calm under pressure at work?

Demonstration of core values. Promotion of people who do not manifest the company's values (e.g. respect for the individual, team working) produces deep cynicism among the staff. Check carefully for these value-sensitive behaviours.

Evidence of leadership requirements. Assess each leader for the skills and behaviours needed to deliver the company's strategy successfully through observation in the workplace and by using psychometric assessments.

Assessment methods

How do you assess if someone is ready, willing and able to perform a role that they're not yet performing?

There are several methods you can use. Some of the key ones are:

Give them opportunities. One way of assessing a person's ability to perform a role they're not yet performing is to give them the opportunity to step into that role. This allows you to see if they display the skills and behaviours you're looking for, and you can both identify the support they need to develop.

Psychometric assessment. By measuring intellect, emotional intelligence, personality, values, motivators and interests, psychometric testing is able to anticipate how someone will respond in a new role and situation, which helps them define the development and support they need. Research shows that good psychometric tests improve assessment by 30–40%, as long as they are used with care and with a focus on any training or development required.

I find the Hogan LEAD Assessment (http://www.hoganassessments.com/) a particularly helpful tool to look specifically at the behaviours defined during the Envisage phase.

Three-hundred-and-sixty-degree feedback. This provides invaluable data on the impact that an individual has in their current role, highlighting strengths and development areas for any future role. Feedback can help determine whether people delivering good results are doing so through others, or at the expense of those around them.

You need to be strategic in your choice of 360-degree feedback tool to measure what you want to measure. You can develop a customised tool that focuses on the specific behaviours and characteristics you are looking for, but as you can imagine, such an approach needs a huge investment of time and money. Or you can use an off-the-shelf tool that covers the general behaviours important for success in most organisations. That approach is more time- and cost-effective, but you still need to ensure it delivers quality feedback and the behaviours it measures are relevant. And the tool must be reliable and valid.

Career conversations. These can help employees develop the clarity and confidence to share their wishes with the organisation and discuss future career choices.

Assessment centres. These use a range of information sources, such as structured interviews, experience and observation, psychometric tests and 360-degree feedback to provide insights into how people work. The benefit of an assessment centre is that it allows you to assess large numbers of employees quickly and efficiently, using a fair process that provides insights into an employee's strengths and development needs for new roles and situations.

Regardless of which method you choose, the important thing is to assess with care. Ensure you base your assessment on various sources and recognise that it is a snapshot in time. It identifies the person's *current* readiness, willingness and ability to take on new responsibilities, focusing on the development and support they will need to realise their ambitions.

How to develop a robust people plan

If you are going to continue the growth of your organisation, you need a plan to grow and develop your people. My recommendation is for each management team to hold a People Review every quarter. In that People Review, discuss who can take on more challenging roles or specific responsibilities within the company.

The aim of the People Review is to manage four risks to the business:

- ❯ **Vacancy risk** – the risk of someone in a critical role leaving and there being no-one who can step into it

- ❯ **Readiness risk** – the risk that your people won't develop the necessary skills, behaviours and experience to be successful in more challenging roles

- ❯ **Transition risk** – the risk of people struggling with the transition into new roles

- ❯ **Strategic risk** – the risk of people not being able to deliver the business strategy and goals.

The People Review is not just important for the company, it's also important for external investors. High-tech companies often rely on private equity investment before being bought or going public. In either event, they need to provide investors with assurance around their management of risk.

The People Review is an important strategic business discussion, not just an HR process. It needs to involve all members of the management team so they take collective ownership of the People Plan and the actions agreed.

A People Review is a decision-making forum, and those decisions can often be tough ones. The fit between behaviours, ability and strategy may mean reallocating responsibilities. It may even mean parting with some individuals whose profiles no longer fit organisational needs. The People Review asks questions about those currently in critical roles:

❯ Who are our key players?

❯ How are they doing?

❯ What is their career potential?

❯ What are their interests?

❯ What are their strengths, weaknesses, development needs?

❯ What are we doing to help develop them?

❯ Are there any retention risks?

❯ Are we missing any talent?

And potential future leaders:

❯ How might we restructure?

❯ What jobs might we create or cut?

❯ Who are our internal successors?

❯ Are they ready to step up? If not, what are we doing to help develop them?

❯ What are the retention risks (if no bigger job opens up or people are passed over)?

❯ What and how do we develop them for future roles?

People Reviews assess potential. Leadership development is about helping people realise that potential. It's about helping them be ready, willing and able to increase their contribution to the organisation. That will include managing their performance in their current role as well as developing them for future roles. If you don't do anything to develop the people you've assessed, they'll be no more ready to take on a new role in two years than they are today.

Investment in their development improves people's readiness to take on more challenging roles. It also helps keep them in the organisation, building their commitment and engagement.

Summary

In this chapter, we've looked at the two perspectives to consider when assessing leadership: the organisation's need to assess whether people are ready, willing and able to take on leadership roles and the employee's ability, motivation and opportunity to perform effectively in a leadership role. We've learned how to take a more scientific and objective approach to identifying leaders with potential to grow the company, understanding the difference between 'performance' and 'potential'. This all leads on to a robust People Plan for your growing organisation.

 1. Conduct a comprehensive People Review which identifies your talent pool and successors.

2. Put together a robust People Plan that mitigates the four key risks to the organisation.

3. Decide on development strategies and actions to improve leadership readiness and capability.

Chapter Five

Assess Part 2
Career conversations

> *To add value to others, one must first value others.*
>
> JOHN C MAXWELL

I have a confession. Even with decades of leadership development experience, I have let some of my best employees down. Part 2 of the Assess element is about preventing that.

I'll never forget one time when I was working at Avanade. It was only 8.30am, and I was surprised to see one of my best employees, Julie, had already arrived as I was usually the first in.

So I said, 'Good Morning, Julie. You're in bright and early,' as I walked into my office.

Within five minutes, she put her head around the door and said, 'May I have a word, Antoinette?'

Even before I'd finished saying, 'Yes, of course,' she had slid the glass door closed behind her.

Now if you've ever managed people, you'll know that when they ask to see you first thing, it is not normally good news.

Sure enough, Julie said, 'I'm sorry, Antoinette. I need to give you my resignation. I'm going back to Australia.'

My heart sank. I was shocked. I was hurt. I was upset. I hadn't seen it coming. Yes, she was an Australian, but she'd recently married a Brit. She was happy in her work and I'd assumed she was settled in the UK.

That was my big mistake. I'd *assumed* I knew what she wanted from her career. But I'd never had a conversation with her about it, and she had obviously felt unable to share her wishes. It turned out she was thinking about starting a family and she wanted to be close to her parents.

Thankfully, it wasn't too late. The company was global with offices in Australia. We could transfer her to an HR role in the Sydney office. Ten years later, she is still there, has risen to HR Director for all Asia Pacific and has two beautiful daughters.

So the story had a happy ending. But it could have been a much more positive experience for us both if we'd had a career conversation earlier. And, as her manager, it was down to me to start that conversation.

That's the focus of this chapter. How can you help employees take ownership of their career development?

Conversations about future leaders' careers

It's a competitive environment, and high-tech organisations need to gain advantage through their people more than ever. People are the key to business success, and research shows engaging employees boosts performance by 15–30%.

But there's a challenge. While organisations want to maximise employees' *performance*, employees want to maximise their *careers*. And these goals are not one and the same.

High-tech companies are under increasing pressure to grow quickly. That leads to expanding roles, increased workloads and changing organisations, all of which can feel hugely punishing to employees.

Employees at all levels face career decisions every day: is my job safe? Should I stay or should I leave? Should I change careers? Should I pursue new projects? Should I go back to university? Should I start up on my own? In a rapidly changing work environment, the answers are not always obvious.

Employees don't care about your organisation. They care about their careers.

OK, that's a provocative statement. I should say 'employees don't care about your organisation *as much as* their careers'. But I don't want to dilute the point. Meaningfulness of work and the fit between a person and their job are two of the key drivers of engagement at work.[1]

Sadly, all the changes fast-growing organisations make are supposed to be a means to an end. They're intended to

---

1   CIPD (2010), 'Creating an Engaged Workforce'.

help the company succeed in a competitive environment, developing an organisation that will thrive and continue to grow. More than ever, organisations need to hold on to their people and develop them for the future. But even if they take steps to manage talent, plan for succession and develop their employees, they often do it behind closed doors in the rarefied atmosphere of the CEO's office or Boardroom. In other words, they take a top-down 'organisation-focused' approach, not recognising their future leaders are taking a bottom-up approach to managing their careers.

The key to engaging and keeping your best people is to help them develop their careers in line with the needs of the business. The most important step you can take is to show you care about your employees by talking to them about their careers.

It's like any relationship – you show you care through conversation. When managers don't have career conversations with their employees, the business relationship becomes like an unhappy marriage where the couple no longer talk to each other about anything meaningful. Next thing you know, one of them has packed their bags or moved into the spare room.

The same happens with employees if their career needs aren't met. They quit physically and leave. Or worse, they quit psychologically and stay.

Let me share a story of why this is important.

Before I set up my own business, I worked for a global insurance company as the Leadership and Organisation Development (LOD) Director. And I was responsible for the talent management process.

After months of preparation, it was time to chair the Talent Review meeting. Our aim was to agree the Succession Plan for the Executive Board.

As is usual in these kinds of meetings, the incumbents of various senior roles sat around a Board table, their task being to slot names into the boxes on the Succession Plan, while my job was to facilitate the discussion and encourage challenge and debate.

The Board agreed most names easily, but a minority caused much discussion. For example, the suggested successor for the Head of Property Underwriting in London was a well-respected Underwriter in the Bermudian office, and there was full agreement about his ability and potential. As always, I asked how the employee in question would feel about such a move. His manager's response?

'Don't worry, love. He'll be made up. He's a good, ambitious bloke. His wife doesn't work and his kids aren't at school yet, so there won't be any issue with him moving to London.'

Six months later, the Head of Property Underwriting left the company as part of a reorganisation. So, his successor got the fated tap on the shoulder. And how do you think he responded?

He said, 'No thanks. I've never wanted the management responsibility that comes with being a head of department, and my wife won't leave her family in Bermuda.'

The whole succession plan fell over because it hadn't considered the career wishes of the employee involved.

If you've ever been on the receiving end of a job move that you didn't want or expect, you'll know how he felt. You may also empathise with what the employee did next – he decided that since the company clearly had a different view of his future to his own, he would be better off leaving.

It is hard to predict the true cost of a departing employee. There are many intangible and often untracked costs associated with employee turnover. A study by the Center for America Progress concluded the cost of losing an employee can be anywhere from 16% of the annual salary of an employee paid hourly to 213% of the salary of a highly trained position[2]. So if we assume the Bermudian Property Underwriter was making $100,000 a year, the true loss could be up to $213,000 to the company. All for the lack of a short conversation about careers.

This story is only too common, and it highlights a major risk: if you don't talk to employees about their careers, you can't take their ambitions into account. And if you don't consider those ambitions in your talent management and leadership development programmes, you could be wasting your time and energy.

Why Performance Reviews are *not* the place for career conversations

Some people may have read that last section feeling confident that their organisation isn't making that mistake. After all, as part of the Performance Review, they ask employees, 'What are your career goals?'

I'm sorry to say that approach doesn't work.

If you have them to hand, take a look at some completed

---

2   Center for American Progress (2012), 'There Are Significant Business Costs to Replacing Employees'.

Performance Reviews. How many times is that question answered? One HR Business Partner told me that in her case, the question was left blank in at least 80% of cases. In the other 20% of cases, the reply was a generic statement like 'To be promoted'.

So why don't employees answer the question?

Research for the Department for Business, Innovation and Skills confirms what I know instinctively – career choices and decisions are complex[3]. They're influenced by many factors, both internal and external. A question such as 'What are your career goals?' is simple to ask, but not at all simple for most people to answer. Not unless they have done a lot of thinking about it beforehand.

Even if they can answer the question, the end of a Performance Review is not the time to tackle such a complex subject. A Performance Review focuses on an employee's *past* performance over a period of time. The emphasis is on the employee's accomplishments relative to specific standards set by the organisation. A career discussion, on the other hand, focuses on their *future*. The emphasis is on the skills and abilities needed to achieve their personal career goals. Managers and employees need to be having career conversations separate from the Performance Review.

So how can you help employees think through their aspirations? How can you help them determine what they want to share with their manager? How can you help them prepare for that conversation?

Let's look at that next.

---

3   Department for Business, Innovation and Skills (2013), 'Adult Career Decision-Making: Qualitative Research'.

What makes a career conversation effective?

It's a sad fact that people can usually identify a memorably bad career conversation, but it's often hard for them to recall a career conversation which was of significant value to them. Many will remember being asked by their boss at the end of a not particularly glowing performance appraisal where they want to be in five years, to which the honest answer would have been 'Anywhere but here working for you.'

This is why I ask people in my Career Conversations Workshops to think about a valuable career conversation they've had. Then we draw out the characteristics that made that conversation so effective. The following come up time and time again:

They're not necessarily with 'the boss'. The fundamental priority of the most effective career conversations is that the person taking them is objective. They must have the best interests of the employee at heart and no underlying agenda.

For these reasons, career conversations can be difficult for the immediate line manager to take. Eventually, career conversations do need to take place between employees and their managers, but that might be the place to finish rather than start the conversation.

They take place informally. Good career conversations often take place outside any formal management or HR process. Or they may take place in what I call 'semi-formal' settings, such as mentoring discussions, regular progress meetings or follow-up meetings after an appraisal. Although good conversations can take place as part of formal HR processes, they're not all that frequent.

They are unplanned. Some good career conversations are planned, but they can also be spontaneous. Valuable conversations with friends and work colleagues, for example, often happen spontaneously.

They don't take a long time. Good career conversations usually take time, say three-quarters of an hour to an hour. But a short first conversation can be useful as a prelude to setting up a longer meeting. Sometimes a single conversation can be pivotal; sometimes people need several conversations to make progress

They provide different levels of support at different times. Employees often need career support at defining points in their career, for example, when they're starting a new role, considering a job move or coming to the end of a development programme. At other times they need a lighter touch.

Most of all, career conversations must be all about the employee and what they want from their working life. They have to feel the focus is on them and that their future hasn't already been decided by others.

How to have a great career conversation

Focus on who the employee is, what they want and why. A good career conversation cuts through the noise to help employees focus on where they're at and reduce unnecessary stress. Discussing how they feel about their current job and career clarifies matters, which can help them unload negative emotions.

Help them reflect on their experience. What skills do they like to use? What activities do they enjoy most? What are their values in relation to work? What work environment do they prefer? What people do they enjoy working with?

Enable them to gain clarity of direction. In an effective career conversation, people will reflect on what their ambitions really are. What does success look like for them? Helping them connect their personal values and career wishes, you ignite their passion, which triggers the desire to develop.

Develop self-awareness by holding up a mirror. Good career conversations build confidence. Hold up a mirror so individuals can reflect on their skills and performance, thinking about the feedback they've received from others in the organisation. They then identify what their strengths and weaknesses are themselves. Done well with a positive focus, that helps them believe in their own ability.

Enable a change of perspective. An effective career conversation challenges individuals to think differently, helping them move out of their comfort zone and consider what opportunities are available to them. Those opportunities might be in their current role or elsewhere in the organisation.

Aid their decision making. Quality career conversations help individuals evaluate different alternatives and opportunities, look at the pros and cons and make a decision. Or at least gain greater clarity about where they want to go and the development they need to get there.

Build networks and organisational understanding. People often need support in navigating the processes and politics of the organisation. Career conversations can help them develop an understanding of how things are done 'around here' and decide how to raise their profile and be more visible to key people. And they can help them work out how to crack the system for moving to a different role, if that's what they want to do.

End with action. Good conversations usually lead to action, focusing on the 'What...?' What career development strategies can employees use to make progress? What actions can they take? They'll also agree how they're going to check in and review progress.

Conversations in short periods of time

Quality career conversations are based on powerful questions.

Let me give you an example. One of my clients, Ian, had worked in the Technology Sector for many years. He was in a fast-growing division with lots of pressure from equity partners, the company was going through change, there were all sorts of staff issues and he was tired. He was coming up to sixty and thinking about taking retirement. But he was torn.

I said to him, 'Suppose we wave a magic wand and transport forward in time to your perfect retirement party. What would people be saying about you in their speeches?'

We spent the best part of an hour exploring that question, focusing on the different people who would be at the party – his bosses, colleagues, team members, clients, friends and family.

At the end, he said, 'You know what? I'm not finished yet. It is hard and it is tiring, I've achieved a lot, but there are still a couple of things I want to make happen if I'm going to leave a legacy. I think I've got a lot to offer to those with less experience. Reminding myself of why I do this work has excited me.'

That's the power of a good question.

The most powerful questions are strengths based and solution focused. In other words, they specifically ask about positives. What does the employee like about their current role? What would they like to do more of? What strengths do they feel they bring? What value do they contribute to the organisation? Such questions provoke reflection, insight, ideas and action. They keep the focus on the employee while helping them see things differently. And they encourage them to take ownership of their own development. They help them recognise possibilities. They encourage them to create many alternatives and achievable action steps to build on their knowledge of how to progress.

Career conversations explore three parts of the employee's career journey:

Where they've come from. Marshall Goldsmith famously said, 'What got you here won't get you there.' Well, I would disagree – at least in part. I think what got your potential leaders to their current position *will* help them make further progress.

Help employees identify what they already know about developing their careers in the organisation. Help them look back to understand where they've been and what they've learned along the way. And help them to reflect on what they're good at, what's most important to them, what keeps them engaged and how they like to work.

Most people have forgotten the skills and abilities they have at their disposal, but are strongly aware of what's missing. So they need your help in identifying and focusing on all the resources they have.

Ask questions like:

> ❯ What useful experiences have helped you get where you are today?

❯ What valuable skills have you developed?

❯ What qualities have helped you make progress?

❯ What unique talents set you apart from others?

This is where you can provide useful input. Recall all the success stories you've heard. Give genuine feedback about the positive skills, qualities, behaviours and attitudes of the employee that you've noticed.

Where they're going. Career development is a journey, not a destination. Help employees discover the general direction they want to go in and the variety of routes to get there.

Success means different things to different people. It doesn't have to mean moving up in an organisation. It doesn't have to mean taking on more responsibility.

Career conversations can help employees develop a picture of future success that is meaningful to them.

When I talk about future success, people sometimes think I mean career goals or objectives. I don't. Future success goes beyond goals and objectives to imagine what working life will be like *after* employees have achieved them.

People too often describe success by a position or title – 'I want to be....' – which limits choices and possibilities. Much more helpful is to move past the job title to what they want their experience at work to involve, which opens all sorts of possibilities.

One of my clients, Adrian, experienced this with two members of his team. The two employees in question both said they wanted to be Account Managers. The problem was there was only one Account Manager role and it was already filled.

I encouraged him to ask each team member about their picture of future success. Next time we met, I asked him how he'd got on.

He said, 'Sonia talked about working more closely with clients. She wants experience of managing the team responsible for developing the whole project. She also wants to do more to develop the agency and how it's run. She's ambitious, and that's great because I can give her opportunities to do all those things to a greater or lesser extent in her current role.'

What about the other team member?

'Natalie said she just wants more money. There's nothing much I can do about that. I think she's considering taking a year off to go travelling.'

Help employees to describe in detail how life will be when they have achieved their ambitions. At this stage, it doesn't matter if the ambition is seemingly realistic or not. The purpose of the discussion is simply to fix career direction so employees can explore the many different ways to get to their destination. The choices available to them may include a change in role upwards or sideward, but the greatest opportunities come from finding ways to help them develop in their current role.

Immediate Action. The purpose of a career conversation is to drive action *by the individual.* Help employees identify small changes and actions that can make big differences. By focusing on the immediate future, you can encourage them to commit to doable actions which will help them make progress. By identifying small manageable steps to do immediately, they can direct their energy towards implementation. And that creates enthusiasm for action. Small steps can result in large progress.

Let me close this chapter with a story of how this can work in practice. At the insurance company I mentioned before, we had a Global Development Programme for our high potential junior employees. This year-long programme started with a three-week boot camp at the company's headquarters in Bermuda. During that time, employees worked in teams on projects that would add value to the business, coming back together periodically for project meetings and skills building. The programme ended with a series of presentations to the great and good in the oak panelled Boardroom of the head office.

It was a huge investment in time, effort, resource and money to develop the future leaders of the company. The problem was that after completing the programme, 30% of the graduates left.

One potential casualty was a young man called Andreas. He was a Deal Administrator, a role that he'd already held for three years, and at the end of programme party, he confessed to me that he felt stuck in that role. He didn't want to leave the company, but he felt he might have no choice, and was pleased he'd been on the programme because it would look good on his CV.

The following year, we set up a career management strategy, running workshops to help the graduates think through their careers and take ownership of influencing them. They came together in peer coaching groups to support one another, we trained their managers in how to have career conversations, and we gave them mentors who were part of the leadership talent pool.

Now I left the company not long afterwards so I can't take credit for the success of this strategy. But my successor took the baton and carried on all the work I'd started, and then proudly told me when he hired me to deliver the training workshops and coaching that retention had significantly improved.

And I was delighted to get an update on LinkedIn from Andreas recently. He's still with the company and now has a global role as a Strategy Manager.

Remember, employees don't care about your business, they care about their careers. Talk to them about what they're looking for so you can connect their ambitions to the needs of the organisation. That way you're more likely to keep your best people and develop them into the leaders of the future.

Summary

In this chapter, we've looked at helping leaders take ownership of their career development and why career conversations are important. We've covered what makes a career conversation effective, including ideas about how to have engaging conversations in short periods of time.

If your company is missing the link between a top-down organisation-focused approach to leadership development and a bottom-up employee-focused approach to career development, here are five questions to get you started:

1. What are you doing to empower employees to develop their careers in the organisation?

2. Do employees have the knowledge and skills to manage their careers within the organisation rather than outside it?

3. How often do managers engage in career conversations with employees?

4. How confident are managers to have career conversations?

5. Are you taking employee ambitions into account in your people processes? Think about People Reviews, Succession Management and Development Planning.

Chapter Six

Develop

Proven strategies for developing key people

Contrary to the opinion of many people, leaders are not born. Leaders are made, and they are made by effort and hard work.

VINCE LOMBARDI

I f leadership development is to be effective, it needs a lot more to it than just development programmes. Still, the Develop component is critical.

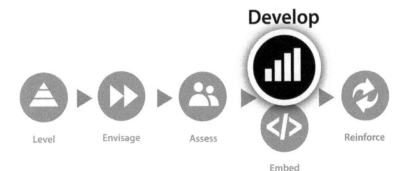

Sustaining growth requires constant change in business direction, management structures, employee workloads and skill requirements. Remaining competitive – even surviving – will depend on the company developing the leaders that it needs to be successful. The trouble is that with things changing on an almost daily basis, it's hard to know where to start in developing leaders for an uncertain future. And you certainly can't afford for your most talented people to be away from the business for extended periods, even if it is for a good reason like developing their leadership skills.

It doesn't have to be that way. This chapter will show you how to design an accelerated solution to develop your leaders' skills as and when they and the business need them. Contrary to popular wisdom, we're going look at why 'training' isn't always the best choice. And we'll look at when it is appropriate to provide support through formal learning.

I'll share with you three steps you can follow to make development effective and rewarding. And we'll discuss the powerful role coaching and mentoring play in developing leaders.

Why training isn't always the best choice

A fast growing business will need to embrace higher levels of change than more established companies. And it'll need leaders who thrive on the unique challenges posed by growth. They'll need to be capable of adapting and continually developing themselves as well as the organisation.

As the business grows and leaders' roles grow with it, they'll need to develop people leadership skills. They may also need to develop functional and organisational leadership skills, depending on their role and position within the organisation.

Companies that excel at developing leaders tend to achieve higher long-term profitability.[1,2] Traditional approaches to leadership development focus on establishing career paths, the organisation typically defining a set of competencies that state what skills and behaviours are expected in a specific role at a particular hierarchical level. The competency framework then forms the basis of a curriculum of leadership training.

A structured approach like this works for stable, bureaucratic organisations where the pace of change is slow and the future skills needed by the organisation can be predicted and mapped out. Unfortunately, it doesn't work well in high-growth, high-change organisations. By nature, they are emergent and dynamic, and the competencies required by leaders will evolve and change just as the organisation does.

That might explain why only 7% of senior managers polled by a UK business school think that their companies develop leaders effectively.[3] And a 2009 survey by the American Society for Training and Development suggests only 14% of Succession Planning and Talent Management Programmes are considered a success. Frankly, experience tells me things

---

1   Robert Gandossy, Marc Effron (2004), *Leading the Way: Three Truths from the Top Companies for Leaders*.
2   Center for Creative Leadership (2014), 'Blended Learning for Leadership: The CCL Approach'.
3   Ashridge Business School (2009), 'Developing the Global Leader of Tomorrow'.

haven't improved over the last few years. Whatever the figure, there's plenty of opportunity for improvement.

Increasingly, we've recognised that leadership development is a process that takes place over time. It's not the outcome of a single event. And the process needs to be integrated with day-to-day work.

Most traditional leadership development programmes are designed in modules. They involve a series of training sessions followed by action projects to transfer the learning back into the workplace.

But that's not the case in a high-growth, high-change organisation which needs to allow leaders to improve their performance immediately with minimal interruption to the business.

I'm going to share with you how to do that.

Three steps to effective development

Business results, business change and business success all stem from the behaviour of individuals. If your leaders are going to develop their leadership skills, they need to experiment with small changes in behaviours.

Even after very basic training sessions, adults typically retain just 10% of what they hear in classroom lectures. That compares to nearly two-thirds when they learn by doing. Furthermore, even talented leaders often struggle to transfer off-site experiences into changed behaviour.

So it is critical to stop seeing leadership development as something that is separate to the business. Instead, it's about putting the leader and the challenges they're facing at the heart of the development activity. That way they develop their leadership ability at the same time as they address the challenges and grow the business. It is during the challenging times that a leader learns most.

Think back on your formative experiences. Did you develop more in the training room or from your experience in the workplace?

Every interaction, every conversation, and every piece of work is an opportunity for leaders to develop their skills. As they manage and grow the business and deliver value for clients and stakeholders, they will develop the leadership skills to help them reach higher performance.

In essence, that means turning the workplace into the classroom, intentionally designing roles and assignments to create development opportunities. It also means providing the support and resources to help leaders extract the learning from their experience. And it means providing access to formal learning, as and when leaders need it, in ways that they can integrate into their working lives. All in all, it makes the workplace more innovative.

That's what I call **Accelerated Leadership Development.**

But of course it's not quite as simple as that. Some leaders tackle challenges every day, but that doesn't necessarily mean they become better leaders.

You need three elements to be in place for Accelerated Leadership Development to be effective.

Focus on developing one or two key leadership skills at a time. Accelerated Leadership Development relies on the leader being highly focused. They concentrate on the specific leadership skills they wish to develop and the actions they're taking to develop them.

This means the starting point of the Accelerated Leadership Development Model is to focus. The leader identifies one or two key leadership skills that will really make a difference to their performance. Then they identify the work tasks and experiences which will give them the opportunities to develop those skills.

Let's consider my client, Tarek. Tarek is the HR Director of a fast-growing online travel company that has ambitious growth plans for the next two to three years.

His biggest leadership challenge was to develop the capability of his direct reports. He needed them to take actions without him having to manage everything. The current situation was limiting the performance of his team and its ability to serve a growing business.

In discussion, we agreed that the most appropriate experience to develop his leadership skill was for Tarek to limit his hours. He was only contracted to work four days a week, but he had found himself regularly working on his day off and at weekends.

Facilitate reflection and feedback. Ensure that leaders make the most of these experiences. They need opportunities to understand what they've learned and how they came to learn it. Quality conversations with peers, coaches and mentors are critical to this process. They support reflection, provide feedback and add just-in-time information.

For Tarek, a key part of his development programme was coaching by me. We spent a fair bit of time discussing what would be different if he was successful in developing the capability of his direct reports. We explored what the benefits of that would be to him, his team and the organisation. We also explored what skills and experience he already had that he could build on.

By discussing examples of how his team managed when Tarek went on holiday, we were able to identify many small actions and behaviours he could try in the normal course of work. He recognised that he had a tendency to 'rescue' his staff when there were problems, driven by a desire to be helpful as well as his high commitment to the role. But he realised it would be better in the long term if he helped them solve the problems for themselves.

Provide access to supporting knowledge, information and formal learning. When the leader knows what experience will develop a leadership skill, they can identify what they need to learn. This will determine what workshops, eLearning, books, etc. will comprise the training element of any leadership development plan.

In agreeing that Tarek needed to help his team solve problems for themselves, we identified that this meant he had to develop his own coaching skills. As a highly experienced HR person, Tarek had good interpersonal skills, but he lacked knowledge of coaching models and frameworks. I shared with him a solutions-focused coaching framework that I use to train people and directed him to various resources.

ACCELERATED LEADERSHIP DEVELOPMENT MODEL

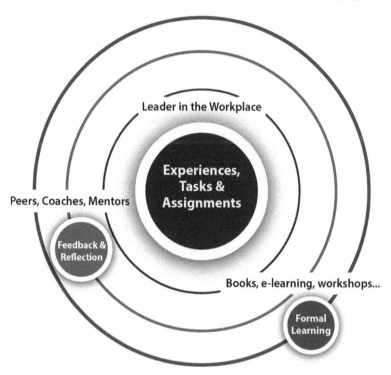

This approach is derived from a concept known as 70:20:10 based on research by Morgan McCall, Robert W. Eichinger and Michael M. Lombardo at the Center for Creative Leadership in North Carolina.[4]

The 70:20:10 concept says that, for any area of development, we learn according to the following ratio: 70% from practical experiences and doing things, 20% from conversations and relationships (coaching, mentoring, supervision, etc.), and 10% through formal training inputs (workshops, eLearning, etc.).

---

4   Center for Creative Leadership (2014), 'Blended Learning for Leadership: The CCL Approach'.

So that's Accelerated Leadership Development in practice. No long, drawn-out training programmes. No guesswork over the full set of skills Tarek would need in the long-term future. Just simple identification of the leadership skills that would have the biggest impact on his performance *right now*. And just-in-time coaching to help him develop those skills.

Over the next few sessions that we worked together, I continued to help Tarek reflect on the progress he made. We discussed what actions he had taken that had helped and what lessons he had learned about leadership and developing his team. He reported that he spent less time on problems and didn't feel he had to work on his days off and at weekends. Instead, he was able to use his new-found coaching skills to get others to think for themselves. And he helped them recognise the skills and knowledge they had to move things forward.

Things were still a challenge and everyone was working hard, but he had noticed a positive impact on ability and action in his team.

Coaching and mentoring

The heart of Accelerated Leadership Development is the leader's experience in the workplace. You need to ensure that leaders make the most out of those experiences, helping them focus on what they need to learn from the experience, then reflect on what they have learned and how they came to learn it.

As well as reflection, they need feedback. Most leaders can't fully see themselves. They may be partly aware of their leadership styles and their varying degrees of leadership skill, but they are rarely aware of their impact on others. Feedback provides them with a mirror that gives them a new perspective about themselves. It allows them to act with greater confidence and develop new ways of approaching things.

So, peers, coaches and mentors are critical.

Peers. Working with peers enables leaders to share experiences and gain confidence that they are not alone in dealing with the daily problems and challenges of leadership. Conversations are a way that leaders can make sense of their experiences. Exchanging ideas and possibilities adds richness to the learning.

Coaches. As illustrated in the scenario with Tarek, coaching can play a valuable role in developing future leaders. A skilled and experienced coach will encourage critical reflection and introspection. They will help leaders prepare for the development experience by talking about:

❯ The key leadership skills that would have the greatest impact on their performance

❯ The experiences/tasks/projects/assignments that will allow them to develop those skills and behaviours

❯ The knowledge and skills they already have to help them and any gaps they need to address.

And they will reflect on the experience by helping leaders think through:

❯ What went well and what feedback they've had from others

❯ What they've learned

❯ How they can build on any progress and continue their development.

Providing coaching to support the development of future leaders is a key role for all existing leaders. But the reality is that it is done with variable results. I recommend you use external coaches or train your leaders in the coaching skills they will need.

Mentors. Richard Branson says, 'If you ask any successful business person, they will always have had a great mentor at some point along the road.'

When I look back on my own career, I have to agree. I can name some key individuals who have been mentors to me and helped me achieve my success. And I still have mentors whom I value.

Different people have different ideas about what mentoring is. I would sum it up by saying, 'Mentoring allows you to share and learn from experience (your own and others').'

Mentoring is an invaluable element of Leadership Development. And it's not just the individuals who benefit from mentoring. The mentors benefit too, as shown below.

BENEFITS OF MENTORING

Mentees have found that mentoring has:	Mentors report the following benefits for themselves:
❥ Guided them around major procedural obstacles and pitfalls ❥ Significantly influenced their attitudes and professional outlook ❥ Widened their professional networks ❥ Enhanced their training and career development ❥ Improved their performance and results by challenging their assumptions	❥ Personal recognition of knowledge, skills and achievements ❥ Satisfaction from helping others and seeing them progress – a chance to give back ❥ Deeper and broader knowledge of their own and other organisations ❥ Increased self-confidence ❥ Higher visibility within the profession ❥ Opportunity to practice and develop management skills ❥ The chance to build wider networks ❥ Job enrichment

Source - Case Study: Workforce Analytics at Sun (Gartner 2006).

And that translates through to benefits for the organisation – 77% of companies report that mentoring programmes are effective in increasing employee retention and performance.[5] And 62% of employees who have received mentoring say they are likely to stay with their current employer.[6]

Good mentors are 'leaders of leaders'. They will use their one-to-one discussions – formal and informal – to share their knowledge of leadership and encourage others to reflect on their experiences. But not all mentors are good leaders, so they must be carefully selected. They need to be trained in such things as listening and storytelling (if they do not come by these qualities naturally). And they need to be carefully matched with future leaders in a non-bureaucratic way. That is not simply on the basis of age or rank, but with regard to the specific leader and the lessons they wish to learn.

As John Buchan, a former Governor-General of Canada, once said, 'The task of leadership is not to put greatness into people but to elicit it, for the greatness is there already.'

Training and Information Support

The third element of the Accelerated Leadership Development Model is for the leader to determine what knowledge, information or formal learning they need, either before engaging in the workplace experience or to address a gap identified as a consequence of the experience.

Leadership skills have traditionally been built through face-to-face development. But, over the last few years, there has

---

5   Christina A Douglas (1997), *Formal Mentoring Programs in Organizations: An Annotated Bibliography.*
6   Source: Yellowbrick.

been a considerable increase in the use of technology.[7] This is particularly important as Accelerated Leadership Development requires leaders to access knowledge as and when they need it. Today's leaders still need formal training that is built around specific leadership skills. But, the interactive nature of today's business climate transforms the model of leadership training from classroom-based to a significant amount of online resources. It may also involve social and mobile tools.[8]

Leadership training must include 'high-touch' activities to be effective. In Accelerated Leadership Development, that high-touch is achieved through coaching and mentoring. So, technology-based training can often be used to address the information needs in bite-sized chunks. That way they can be integrated into the working day.

ONLINE LEARNING METHODS

❯ Webinars	❯ Video content of best practice
❯ Teleseminars	outside the organisation
❯ Immersive learning	❯ External social networking
environments e.g. games	or Peer-to-Peer sites (e.g.
and simulations	Facebook, LinkedIn, Twitter)
❯ Podcasts	❯ In-house social media
❯ Video conferencing/virtual	❯ Dedicated online resources
presence	for leadership e.g. Harvard
❯ Interactive E-learning courses	ManageMentor, ILM,
❯ Delivery of content via mobile	LearningZone, CMI
devices (mLearning)	❯ Other online resources such
❯ Video content of best practice	as eBooks and eJournals
within the organisation	❯ Leadership blogs

---

7   Towards Maturity (2010), 'Accelerating Performance – Towards Maturity 2010–2011 Benchmark'.

8   Bersin & Associates Research Bulletin (2012), 'Integrated Talent Management: A Roadmap for Success'

In general conversation, many leaders still express a preference for face-to-face leadership development programmes. Yet studies show that when they're exposed to new media, that preference for pure classroom training diminishes.

Summary

In this chapter, we've looked at why training isn't always the best choice. Instead, there's Accelerated Leadership Development. Its three strategies work together to help you develop leaders' skills as and when they and the business need them, focusing on the one or two key leadership lessons that will really make a difference to performance. You can then plan the experiences and work tasks which will give leaders the opportunities to learn those lessons.

We've also examined the power of coaching and mentoring to facilitate feedback and reflection, helping leaders understand what they've learned and how they came to learn it. And we've talked about when and how to provide access to knowledge, information or formal learning.

By embracing a wide range of formal, informal, on-demand and experiential learning methods, you can provide learning as and when leaders need it.

How do you design an Accelerated Leadership Development Solution for your organisation? Start by asking yourself these questions:

❯ What is the leadership lesson that will have the greatest impact on the leader's performance?

❯ What experiences/tasks/projects/assignments will allow them to learn that leadership lesson?

❯ If they are successful in learning that leadership lesson, what will be different? What will be the benefits?

❯ What knowledge, skills and experience do they already have that will help them?

❯ What will they need to learn before they engage in those experiences/tasks/projects/assignments?

❯ What resources are available to help them gain the knowledge and information they need?

In fast-growth, fast-change organisations, things need to move *fast*. So don't worry about getting a whole development journey mapped out. It's important to be clear on the direction in which development must occur, then focus on the immediate steps and review them regularly.

Chapter Seven

Embed

Helping leaders adopt new skills and behaviours

Leadership is practiced not so much in words as in attitude and in actions.

HAROLD S. GENEEN (American businessman most famous for serving as president of the ITT Corporation)

One of the biggest concerns I hear is, 'How do we get leaders to transfer learning from development programmes into the workplace?'

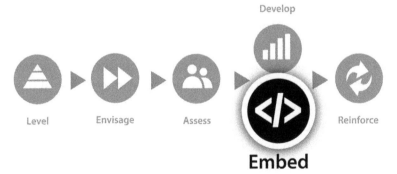

To develop effective leaders in your company, you need to create behavioural change in your people. And that can be a challenge. Just because a person knows why they need to change their behaviour and learns the steps for doing it doesn't mean they will. Are there things you know you shouldn't do, but you keep doing them anyway? They might be behaviours such as not speaking up at meetings or constantly overworking to the detriment of your family.

The Embed component of the LEADER system runs in parallel with the Develop component to ensure new leadership behaviours become part of the day-to-day practice in the workplace. In this chapter, we'll look at how to motivate leaders to change their behaviour in the first instance, and how to make it easy for them to do so. And I'll outline how you can design development programmes to make the new behaviour become a habit.

Three ways to create sustained behaviour change

Some of the most significant insights into behaviour change come from Stanford University. In the Persuasive Tech Lab, Dr B. J. Fogg and his team research how we can change undesired behaviour into desired behaviour.

Fogg suggests that behaviour and behaviour change is not as complicated as most people think[1]. It's systematic, straightforward and simple. His 'BJ Fogg Behavior Model' proposes that three elements must come together at the same moment for a behaviour to occur: the motivation for that behaviour, the ability to perform the behaviour, and a trigger. When a wanted leadership behaviour does not occur, it's likely that at least one of those three elements is missing.

1   B. J. Fogg (2014), 'Top 10 Mistakes in Behavior Change'.

Motivation

Q. How many psychologists does it take to change a light bulb?

A. One, but the light bulb has to want to change.

Unless someone is willing to commit to a new goal, they are unlikely to make lasting changes in their leadership behaviour. They won't take actions that will help them achieve that goal and turn it into a habit. So, the first thing to focus on is a leader's motivation to change.

In his best-selling book *Drive*, Daniel Pink highlights research into motivation. He states that it stems from purpose, mastery and autonomy. In situations where people are paid fairly, this trio drives, engages and stimulates them to do their best work[2].

DRIVERS OF MOTIVATION

Based on DRIVE by Daniel Pink

---

2   Daniel H. Pink (2010), *Drive: The Surprising Truth About What Motivates Us*.

This is important to me. People who find purpose in their work are the most motivated. Purpose is what gets them out of bed in the morning and into work without groaning and grumbling – something that they can't fake.

For people to change, they need to see that making that change will result in a personal benefit. They need to know what's in it for them – especially as changing their behaviour can be difficult and challenging.

For leaders in the Tech Sector, the insight could be that learning a new skill, which demands energy and effort, will result in them changing the way they manage their team. And that will provide them with more time and less stress – a clear personal benefit.

Or it might be even more personal than that. When I work with any leader on their development, we look at what they want to change and the benefits of making that change. We start with exploring the benefits to them personally, but we then move on to others – their bosses, their team, their peers, even their family.

One leader I worked with was struggling with her confidence and resilience at work as a couple of things hadn't gone well in the past few months. She felt like she couldn't get everything done, was missing deadlines and letting people down.

At one point she started crying, saying, 'I'm so unhappy. I used to love my job, but I feel like I've lost my way and don't know how to get back.'

I could see that she was in danger of spiralling into negativity and despair which would get in the way of her doing what she needed to make progress.

When I asked who else would benefit if she could improve the situation, she got quite animated. She said the main person who would notice would be her husband, because she went home every night and moaned about what she saw as her failings.

She said, 'He's sympathetic, but I can tell he's getting frustrated by my lack of self-confidence.'

She also thought her team would notice. It was a joke among them that when she got stressed, she had 'high hair' because she was always running her hands through it.

That wasn't even our first session, it was just the pre-meeting. But by thinking through who was affected by her behaviour, and how they were affected, she was motivated to do something about it. She even identified some small steps she could take immediately.

I want to get better at this. Mastery describes our natural wish to get better at doing things. It's why learning a language or an instrument can be so frustrating at first. If you feel like you're not getting anywhere, your interest flags and you may even give up. A sense of progress, not just in our work but in our abilities, contributes to our inner drive.

In my experience, talented individuals are motivated to become better leaders. But they need motivation to prioritise their development as a leader and try new ways of doing things rather than carrying on as before.

One way to motivate leaders is to encourage them to paint a vivid picture of the current situation and how things could be different using stories and metaphors. Visualising success can be a powerful force for change. Get them to build physical objects to create an image of 'where we are now' versus 'where we want to be' – a glorious new state. This taps into people's emotions, a forceful lever for motivating change.

It's my idea. Autonomy reflects our natural inclination for self-direction. We're all built with inner drive, so we don't want someone else telling us what to do unless we ask them.

That's why I always co-design development programmes with the leaders who are taking part. It supports autonomy by giving them real control over what they want to change and what skills and behaviours they need to develop.

People rarely change their behaviour because of information. And when it comes to leadership, there is no one right way to behave. What works for one leader in one situation will differ for another leader and a different situation.

The role of a leadership programme is to give leaders a diverse range of new tools. Leaders can then choose which to experiment with to find what works for them.

Ability

After deciding on the action they're going to take, the leader will try out a new way of behaving for the first time. And that experiment is a critical moment.

The biggest mistake leaders make is to try to make huge changes. And then they end up in a vicious loop. Because the change is difficult, they don't feel they are making progress, and that is demotivating so they then stop trying and give up.

To overcome this, the key is to start with small, doable 'baby steps'.

Fogg explains that, 'In most situations behavior change occurs only when the behavior is easy to do.' So, if we want to change our behaviour, we need to start with the small things. It might sound counter-intuitive, but it increases the likelihood of the leader taking action. Once this small behaviour has become a fixed habit through continuous repetition, it is much easier to expand on it.

For example, a leader might say they want to 'improve trust' in their team. That's not a behaviour, that's a result. The small step might be to facilitate information sharing at a team event. Or it might be to create an opportunity for two team members to work together to build their relationship.

One great example of the power of small steps is an initiative carried out by an ex-colleague of mine at Accenture. She wanted to find a way to help leaders view people development as many 'micro-actions' – development on-the-job rather than something separate – so she launched a thirty-day challenge called 'Developing People Is Our Business'.[3]

The challenge consisted of thirty micro-actions (things that take fewer than ten minutes to carry out) designed to build trust, engagement and productivity when applied little and often. Since the challenge needed people to take the actions every day, they needed to be manageable.

The aim was to show that it's the little things that make all the difference. They add up over time, contributing to people's engagement bit by bit.

In the challenge, the micro-actions were sent out one at a time, over a month. Participants who signed up (it was voluntary) would, ideally, take the challenge each day, then comment on the actions they had taken and the impact they'd noticed on themselves, the people around them,

---

3   Accenture (2010), 'Developing Tomorrow's Talent: A girl, a blog and 30 days to business impact'.

and the business. This provided motivation for others to try out the micro-actions if they hadn't already done so.

Everything about the challenge was as easy as possible. It was easy to sign up. It was easy to receive the instructions. And it was easy to complete the micro-actions. As a result, thousands of people signed up from forty-seven different countries. According to feedback, each participant engaged in thirteen challenges and felt they had an impact on an average of seven people because of the challenge.

As these small steps created positive results, people continued to engage in behaviours that improved their communication and developed others. And this delivered business impacts in several extra areas. The largest impact was on people's own engagement. This led to increased opportunities to collaborate with others.

Accenture's thirty-day challenge

Day 1. Think about someone inspiring and tell them what it is about them that inspires you.

Day 2. Ask two people how their days are going and really listen to their replies.

Day 3. Write a note/letter to someone today, perhaps as a thank-you or to say you're thinking about them.

Day 4. Think about a valuable piece of advice that you have been given or learned over the years and pass that advice along to another person.

Day 5. Ask open questions instead of telling someone what to do. See how the other person thrives as your questions enable them to come to their own conclusions.

Day 6. Pay yourself an act of kindness to congratulate yourself on a job well done this week, no matter how great or small.

Day 7. Remember to make eye contact and listen with genuine interest today. You are certain to create a favourable impression if you are fully present in the conversation.

Day 8. Start a team meeting/conference call today with a positive recount of what's going right.

Day 9. Take the time to have a conversation with someone without rushing on to the next task or meeting.

Day 10. Take a colleague to a meeting where they can stretch themselves.

Day 11. Take sixty seconds and three steps to provide on-the-spot positive feedback – (1) tell an employee exactly what they did that was right, (2) tell them what value or goal they achieved, and (3) say thank you.

Day 12. At the end of the day, write down three things that went right this week. Getting into the habit of looking for the positives around you will pay dividends and give you many things to recognise.

Day 13. Do something that scares you today (stretch yourself).

Day 14. Reach out to someone and ask how you might help them.

Day 15. Ask for people's opinion and input on a project. Trusting and acting on their judgement is one of the greatest compliments you can give a person.

Day 16. True trust-building leaders communicate often and well so that people feel 'in on things'. What do you need to over-communicate today?

Day 17. Gossip needs to be shared most with the person about whom you are gossiping. Solve problems through direct communication with the person/people involved.

Day 18. Catch someone doing something right and praise them for it immediately.

Day 19. Complete one piece of people developer documentation that you have been putting off. This could be a performance review, a mid-year review, or a simple email delivering feedback to someone's supervisor.

Day 20. Pass along your favourite inspirational quote today to someone who you think it will help, and explain to them how the quote made you think of them.

Day 21. Pick up the phone or e-mail to schedule a time to catch up with someone you have mentored in the past to see how they are doing.

Day 22. Give people the gift of your time by 'single tasking' today. Commit in at least one meeting to giving the participants your full, undivided attention – no multi-tasking with email, instant messenger, etc. Both you and your colleagues will benefit.

Day 23. Read one article on some aspect of leadership that you would like to improve on. Share with others what you learn and the actions you are going to take as a result.

Day 24. When we think of developing people, we often look down more than we look up. Provide one piece of constructive feedback to your boss today that will enable you to do an even better job.

Day 25. Pick one person with whom you would like to build a more trusting relationship. Disclose something about yourself that might not come up in a typical conversation with them. Listen carefully if they choose to disclose something about themselves in return.

Day 26. If you or someone else makes a mistake today, ask questions that encourage learning.

Day 27. Ask someone to make an introduction to enable you to expand your network.

Day 28. Pay a compliment to at least three people.

Day 29. As you teach someone about the task at hand, describe how it fits into the bigger picture to enable them to see the context within which to make decisions.

Day 30. Come up with your own People Developer-related challenge, and take that challenge.

Trigger

All the suggestions listed above will help a behaviour happen once. But for a behaviour to happen repeatedly so it becomes part of the way a leader works, it needs to become routine rather than 'new'.

The leader's job and how they interact with others is part of their habitual behaviour, their daily routine. So how do you trigger the new desired behaviour rather than the automatic undesired behaviour?

Fogg recommends that you use an existing routine behaviour as the trigger. Sounds complicated? In fact, it's simple.

Here's an example of how it works in a fitness context. A typical approach to getting back into a daily routine of physical exercise might be to commit yourself to a vague new behaviour such as 'I am going to start training, become fit and live more healthily'. Instead, find a daily routine (for example 'after I wake up in the morning') then link that to a simple and easily executable new behaviour (for example 'I will perform three sit-ups'). Just that.

Let's apply the approach to leadership. A new leadership routine might be 'every day when I return from lunch (trigger) I will write a note to thank one person for something they've done well (new behaviour)'. Or 'every week at the beginning of the team meeting (trigger)', I will ask team members to share their stories of success from the past week (new behaviour).

In the thirty-day challenge, the most popular challenges were those that were already part of people's work routine. They simply needed a tweak in that routine. Of course, once the new behaviour is embedded, you can then build up the challenge, encouraging people to take the next small step.

Marshall Goldsmith is author of the book *Triggers: Creating Behavior That Lasts – Becoming the Person You Want to Be.*[4] In it he describes the triggers he uses himself for productive, beneficial change, which are a set of questions directly related to the specific leadership skills he wants to develop that he has designed and chosen himself. Every

---

4   Marshall Goldsmith and Mark Reiter (2015), *Triggers: Creating Behavior That Lasts – Becoming the Person You Want to Be.*

night, Goldsmith has a friend call him and ask the same set of questions. (Remarkably, they are still friends.)

The questions all start with the phrase, 'Did I do my best [today] to...' and the endings may be strategic ('...set clear goals?'), professional ('...preserve all client relationships?'), philosophical ('...be grateful for what I have?'), physical ('...exercise?'), or personal ('...say or do something nice for Lynda?' [his spouse]).

What I like about this approach is that it combines all three elements that we have discussed in this chapter. It uses motivation – the questions are self-chosen to focus on what the leader wants to develop. It addresses ability – the questions reflect on small steps taken in the last twenty-four hours. And it creates triggers – the questions have become a daily routine.

How to implement the Embed component

To embed new leadership behaviours, build the following five stages into any development activity:

EMBED MODEL

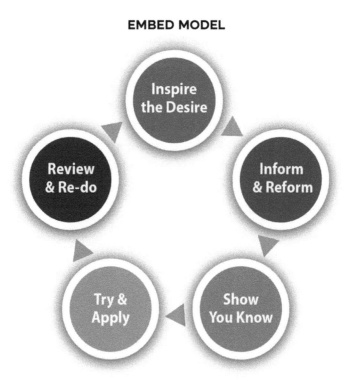

Inspire the desire. Help people see the benefit of changing their behaviour. It's what's referred to as the 'What's in it for me?' factor. You can do this by helping them reflect on what is and is not currently working. Encourage them to identify the benefits of change to them, to their team, to the organisation and to others. Use creative techniques to help them visualise an appealing future after the change has taken place.

Inform and reform. People need to be informed on new ideas around how to act and behave differently. They also need to reform their current thinking and assumptions. Help them look at what they know in new ways, learn new ways of doing things or see others behaving differently to them.

One of the greatest sources for developing leaders is other leaders. Create an environment where leaders can generate ideas, exchange different approaches and share experiences.

Show they know. Give leaders the opportunity to practise and rehearse new actions and behaviours in a safe environment. Giving and getting feedback can be a valuable way of leaders learning together. Another way is using professional actors who can provide an invaluable opportunity for participants to try out new behaviours and develop their skills in a 'real' environment.

Try and apply. Encourage leaders to identify the small steps they will try and apply as a result of the development. And discuss how they are going to reflect on the experience and record the results so they can capture their learning.

Review and re-do. Help leaders identify the triggers and create the routines that will encourage them to repeat effective behaviours.

Summary

In this chapter, we've explored many ideas for designing development programmes to ensure new behaviour follows and is repeated. We've discussed three elements that motivate leaders to change their behaviour – purpose, mastery and autonomy – and we've learned how important it is to use small steps to make the new behaviour as easy as possible. We now know how to help leaders make the new behaviour become a habit, part of their day-to-day work.

 When you source or design development activities and programmes, build in the following practices:

1. Motivate leaders by making the development personal, positive and rewarding. Help leaders identify what's in it for them. Create an environment where they can generate ideas and share experiences. Provide autonomy by involving leaders in the design of the programme.

2. End every development activity with leaders identifying the small steps they are going to try and apply in the workplace.

3. Encourage leaders to set up triggers and routines to create new leadership habits.

Chapter Eight

Reinforce
Developing a culture of growth

I think that the best training a top manager can be engaged in is management by example. I want to make sure there is no discrepancy between what we say and what we do. If you preach accountability and then promote somebody with bad results, it doesn't work. I personally believe the best training is management by example. Don't believe what I say. Believe what I do.

**CARLOS GHOSN
(CEO of Renault-Nissan)**

The final component of the LEADER system is Reinforce. It is just as important as all the other components, but it is all too easily forgotten.

The Develop and Embed components of the system focus primarily on the leaders themselves, their actions and behaviours. But what about the context in which they're operating? Are you fostering an environment that cultivates and empowers leadership from your people?

Creating a culture of leadership is a key ingredient in a company's ability to continue rapid growth year on year, but it is not something that you can just impose. A culture of leadership evolves when you invest time and resources in leaders not only at the top, but throughout your organisation.

In this chapter, we'll discuss five things that great companies do to help create a culture of leadership throughout the organisation. We'll start by looking at how you can give your leaders a clear purpose. We'll then talk about creating a movement around that purpose, learning why it's important to make leadership everyone's responsibility. And we'll explore how to recognise and reward leadership to achieve that. Finally, we'll look at how to remove the obstacles and barriers preventing leadership.

Give your leaders a clear purpose

Organisations with a strong leadership culture communicate their mission, vision and values in a way that brings people together. Their company purpose serves as the compass for everything they do, helping to fuel the work ethic and drive their passion.

To give your leaders a clear purpose, your company vision needs to paint a picture of success that resonates with them. It needs enough direction for everyone to make decisions without seeking permission at every turn and slowing down the process, but must never elicit eye rolling or glazed-over looks. It needs to be genuine, understandable, and compelling.

Six things that make a vision effective

1. It is bold but **achievable**
2. It paints a vivid **picture of the future**
3. It appeals to employees' **hearts** (and minds)
4. It is **specific** enough to help individuals make decisions and trade-offs
5. It is **flexible** enough to adapt to changing conditions
6. It is **easy to communicate** quickly

You also need to publicise and interpret your organisational values. Then everyone knows how the company expects them to behave in striving to realise the vision. Communication needs to be constant, heartfelt and consistent. Discuss the values at every opportunity, and reward those who remember, understand and practise them.

Here's the story of how one company shared its vision with the entire organisation.

A British software company was trying to transform its business and it had created a vision for doing so. Leaders had already communicated the vision, but they wanted to reinforce it, so employees turned on their computers one morning to find a new screen saver – a multi-coloured map of the UK surrounded by a bright blue circle. The words around the circle read, 'We will be #1 in the UK market by 2017.'

Because it appeared on everyone's computer on the same day, they all started talking about it.

'The strangest thing happened when I logged on this morning.'

'Oh, you got one of those new screen savers, too?'

'Did everyone get one?'

The screen saver created a daily routine that triggered two behaviours. Firstly, it reminded individuals of their primary focus. That helped them decide their priorities during their working day. Secondly, it inspired them in meetings to talk about what they could all do to realise the vision in their departments. Over the weeks and months, they talked about more specific metrics. They talked about having five new products in the UK by a certain time, growing at a rate of at least 15% a year, etc. And the leadership periodically updated the screen saver message and metrics.

One senior leader noted, 'I could walk around the office and ask people what last year's results were, and what this year's target is. And many could respond without even having to think about it. These were people who, a year before, might not even have been able to quote the company's vision, let alone its targets. It's amazing what can happen if large numbers of us all understand what the goals are.'

The screen saver worked because it was a constant reminder of the company's goals. Another CEO I know posted the vision on the curved wall of the lift shaft so that it was the first thing everyone saw every morning.

Sharing the vision and goals is just one part of the story, though. We all know of companies who proudly display their organisation values in the hall of their head office. But that means nothing unless those values are lived and breathed by everyone who works for the company.

Take, for example, the company that stated on its website, 'As a global corporate citizen, [the company] intends to conduct itself in accord with four values. Respect, Integrity, Communication, Excellence.'

Which company do you think that might be? Are you surprised to learn it's Enron, the company whose bankruptcy, moral and otherwise, has become infamous? Their values may have been visible in words, but they weren't so visible in behaviour. And it's behaviour that matters.

For the software company, it was important its people behaved in line with its values: Collaboration, Innovation, Customer Focus and Trust. The company knew that it couldn't simply write down what it wanted the values and behaviours to be and expect others to follow. It was critical to reflect a culture of leadership through actions. The senior staff needed to use the values as a regular touch point in decision-making. That ensured people brought them to life every day – not just when it was easy or convenient.

They decided to reinforce the company's values daily and weekly by using storytelling. At the beginning of every meeting, they shared inspiring stories that were examples of the values in practice.

Lay the groundwork for a leadership culture by being clear with your company purpose, then build on it by senior people modelling the behaviours you would like to see practised. Only then can you set up the right structures and processes to foster and reinforce the culture you want.

Create a movement around the purpose

Leading in today's increasingly competitive, accelerated and uncertain world takes courage. Only when leaders display the courage they wish to see in others will they be able to unleash the potential within their teams and organisation. Strong leadership raises the bar on innovation and optimises the value the organisation contributes. It doesn't take the brains of Einstein to do that, but it does take the heart of a lion.

The pace of change in a fast-growing high-tech company is accelerating, so it's more important than ever for people to be willing to step out of their comfort zone. They need the courage to lay their reputation (or even job) on the line and take bold action. Such a culture is one where leaders actively encourage people to challenge status quo thinking. They ask for candid upward feedback. They reward people who experiment and push boundaries.

But how do you create that?

Robert Cialdini, author of *Influence: The Psychology of Persuasion*, talks about the principle of social proof.[1] The principle says that if you don't know exactly what to do, you rely on others around you to help you find the proper way to act. It is a great technique for influencing large numbers of people. And that's exactly what you're trying to achieve when creating a culture.

People copy each other's behaviours because they want to be 'normal'. Most people need to feel that 'people like me act this way, and people I admire and want to be like act this way'. No-one wants to be the odd man out. We live

---

1   Robert B. Cialdini (2007), *Influence: The Psychology of Persuasion.*

in a culture of fear where people face a constant stream of reasons to play safe, keep their mouths shut and disappear underground. Even folks who consider themselves renegades copy renegades they admire.

Social proof works like a chain reaction. Those who are most open and easily persuaded will follow the lead. Others who are less easily persuaded witness this and are then more likely to follow. This can go on until, eventually, the most reluctant individual starts thinking, *everyone else is doing it, so I must be wrong. I'll do it as well.*

There is a great example of this uploaded on YouTube by Derek Sivers called 'First Follower: Leadership Lessons from Dancing Guy'. You can watch it at https://www.youtube.com/watch?v=fW8amMCVAJQ. The video shows a shirtless man dancing alone on a hillside. As Derek Sivers says, he has 'the guts to stand alone and look ridiculous. But what he's doing is so simple, it's almost instructional.'

A second man comes along who follows his lead and joins him dancing on the hillside. Then he calls his friends to join in. Sivers highlights the following lesson:

> *It takes guts to be a first follower! You stand out and brave ridicule, yourself. Being a first follower is an under-appreciated form of leadership. The first follower transforms a lone nut into a leader. If the leader is the flint, the first follower is the spark that makes the fire.*

Within seconds, a third man, the second follower, joins the dance. The voiceover states, 'The second follower is a turning point: it's proof the first has done well. Now it's not a lone nut, and it's not two nuts. Three is a crowd and a crowd is news.'

The video continues showing two more joining, then three more. Now there's momentum. Now they've created a movement.

As more people jump in, it's no longer risky. If people were on the fence before, there's no reason not to join now. No-one will ridicule them, they won't stand out, and they will be part of the in-crowd, if they hurry. Over the next minute we see the rest who prefer to be part of the crowd join in, because eventually they'd be ridiculed for not joining.

When I watched the video, it reminded me of a time shortly after I joined Avanade when I got the opportunity to attend a global Microsoft conference. As I was new to the High-tech Sector, I knew that Microsoft was led by its founder Bill Gates and had partnered with Accenture to co-own the company I now worked for, but I didn't know much about Steve Ballmer, who was President of Microsoft at the time and second to Bill Gates.

At the conference, it became clear to me that Steve Ballmer was critical to Bill Gates's success as a leader. While Gates has been hugely successful, he was known for a leadership style that was authoritarian and abrasive. That is not a style that would inspire people to join him on the hillside. But he wasn't on his own. He had a first follower in Steve Ballmer.

And boy, did employees *love* Steve Ballmer. He was all they could talk about. They couldn't wait to see him, even though his appearance was scheduled for first thing on a Saturday morning. The atmosphere was like a rock concert when Steve Ballmer came on stage – I couldn't believe it.

At the time, Microsoft was in a bitter legal battle over its use of Sun's Java programming language, and it was going to continue to fight. Bill Gates had already made that point in opening the conference the day before. But Steve Ballmer galvanised the crowd behind that message. Before long, he had the whole audience chanting, 'Sun down! Sun down!' It was the workplace equivalent of people rushing to join the dancers on the hillside.

So how can you apply this principle to create a leadership movement in your company? I recommend these steps:

1. Identify your version of the shirtless dancing guy. Who has the guts to stand alone and do something new? Is it the CEO? The Head of Department? Someone completely different?

2. When you've identified them, make sure their leadership is public and easy to follow.

3. Find and nurture the first few followers who are willing to support the movement. They need to be seen to show the leadership you're looking for.

4. Once you have some followers, find and convince the key influencers to help with championing leadership development in the company. They are often not managers with senior titles, but people with the most informal connections. Others look to them for directions. They are well-respected, high-performing and eager people who are displaying leadership through their behaviour.

A movement must be public. Make sure everyone sees more than just the leader. They need to see the followers, because new followers copy followers – not the leader. Use all the communication tools at your disposal to show the followers' leadership in action.

Celebrate the success of role models and focus on their practices to help them gain converts to the new way of behaving.

Make leadership everyone's responsibility

Leadership is not the preserve of a chosen few. And it's not reserved for top management. The success of any organisation depends on how well it can capture the talents of every individual.

To develop a culture of leadership, you need to make sure everyone has some leadership responsibility. Depending on their role, that might be just for leading themselves, or it may be for leading others or the organisation.

Build a culture of leadership into the hiring process. Recruit people who fit with your organisation's idea of leadership. And fix expectations clearly during on-boarding.

One of the things that P&G was famous for (and probably still is) when I joined the company in 1989 was its 'challenging' application form. It was challenging because it tried to identify whether graduates had leadership skills.

The Application Process Brochure still includes the sample question shown below.

Sample Recruitment Question

When organising a work team you select those who:

- ❯ Have different strengths
- ❯ Have the most technical expertise
- ❯ Cooperate with each other
- ❯ Follow instructions
- ❯ Think like you

The process also involves a competency-based interview, including questions looking for evidence of what P&G call

'Success Drivers'. These are specific competencies that define how P&G people succeed in today's business environment. They are also how P&G measures performance in the company.

Examples of Success Factors and Questions

Communication. For example: tell us about a time you had to adjust your communication approach to suit a particular audience.

Decision making. For example: give an example of a time when you had to make a difficult decision.

Leadership. For example: describe a situation when you assumed the role of leader. Were there any challenges, and how did you address them?

Results orientation. For example: give me an example of a time when you were particularly successful.

Teamwork. For example: describe a situation in which you were working as part of a team. How did you make a contribution?

Trustworthiness. For example: give me an example of a time you were deceptive.

No matter what size your organisation is, build leadership behaviours into your recruitment process. And clearly communicate leadership expectations, accountabilities and strategic objectives.

Create collective leadership goals. P&G was also excellent at setting goals for the workforce that guided all employees to display leadership.

When I worked there, I had two sets of performance objectives. The first set related to my job and what I needed to do to 'build the business'. My role as Technical Brand Manager was to develop washing detergents. So my objectives centred on carrying out consumer research, testing different formulations and getting the product ready for launch.

The second set of objectives related to what I could do to 'build the organisation'. That was how I first became involved in people development. I became a Corporate Trainer for the company and trained other managers in interpersonal management skills. I also helped with graduate recruitment by attending recruitment fairs, interviewing candidates and mentoring placement students.

None of these helped me develop a better washing detergent. In fact, they took me away from it, but it is unlikely I would have committed to the organisation if it hadn't set the second objectives as an expectation.

If you want your people to take collective responsibility for growing the business, create collective goals. Set those expectations.

Nurture leadership skills at all levels of the organisation. Successful companies understand the most valuable resource in their organisation is people. They invest in people and help them develop their own leadership capacity. And they scale it throughout the organisation. They have leadership programmes in place at every level, which means employees have access to resources to develop themselves into leaders and improve their leadership abilities.

When I was responsible for leadership development at Accenture, we had several development programmes. We had the Graduate Development Programme for newly hired graduates during their first three years with the company. We had a Leadership Development Programme focused on developing high potential employees to become Partners. And we had development programmes for employees at specific milestones of their career.

Nurturing leaders involves effective and constant feedback to allow employees to flourish. At Accenture, we designed the programmes to identify future stars and start their development early. This gave them opportunities to follow good leadership models and practise their own skills in controlled environments. We also provided training courses, giving leaders the tools to create growth and innovation.

Recognise and reward leadership

For leadership to become a true part of the culture, you need to show that you value it. That means that you need mechanisms in place to recognise and reward the leadership behaviours you want.

Review the 'how' of performance, not just the 'what'. If you recognise and reward only results, you are in danger of encouraging behaviours that are out of line with your values. For example, patients are admitted to hospital simply to ensure the NHS Trust hits its four-hour waiting time target. But such a move ignores the value of patient care.

I saw a similar situation with an insurance company I worked with which wanted to develop its senior leaders. One of the leaders in particular had a dreadful reputation. His team was frustrated, he was famous for never being in the office, and when he was there his style was autocratic, bullying and intimidating. But he was popular with brokers and delivered great deals. If the company looked just at these results, he gave the impression of being a great leader. But the whole picture showed the results wouldn't be sustainable nor support long-term growth of the company.

To develop a culture of leadership, recognise and reward *how* people lead as well as *what* they deliver. And make these criteria essential requirements for progression and promotion

It's not about the money. The subject of reward for leadership is a controversial one. Every year there are news bulletins about fat cat salaries and end of year bonuses. We know money is a motivator, so we expect the more you pay people, the better they perform. And that is true. But only for straightforward tasks.

Dan Pink highlights this in his best-selling book, *Drive*. He makes the point that monetary rewards work for tasks that involve only mechanical skills.[2] But when tasks need knowledge and skills that are less rudimentary, rewards don't work. Leadership needs creative thinking. So I think we can assume that a higher salary won't automatically drive better leadership, which is an assumption that has proved true in my personal experience.

Remove obstacles and barriers

What are the leadership behaviours you'd like to develop within your company? And what are the organisational routines, processes and systems that are your established norms? Can you see a mismatch?

---

2   Daniel H. Pink (2010), *Drive: The Surprising Truth About What Motivates Us.*

With nearly all, if not all the clients I work with, there comes a time when they present various organisation obstacles to leadership: barriers that will get in the way of them behaving how they and the organisation want them to. Those obstacles tend to fall into one of three areas:

❯ The values and behaviours that are displayed in the organisation

❯ HR policies and processes, especially around performance management, recruitment, reward, promotion, training and development

❯ The organisation structure and definitions of roles and responsibilities.

ENABLERS OF LEADERSHIP CULTURE

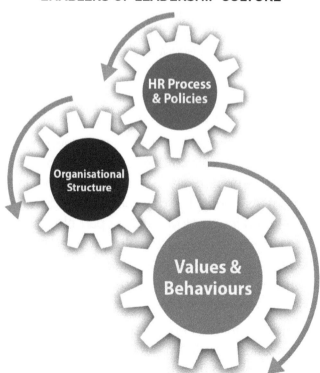

One client company always made me smile when they cited *The Matrix* as the barrier stopping them leading more effectively. I had images of Keanu Reeves dressed in black, trapping my clients in simulated reality just like in the science fiction film. But while it's easy to smile at the idea of an intangible organisation structure getting in the way of leadership, it's a genuine challenge.

I've worked with high-tech companies that want their leaders to develop employees, but then give them personal targets that mean they have no time to focus on anything other than sales and delivery. I've also seen companies that want to develop a culture of collaboration, but then go on to reward employees individually – encouraging competition and not collaboration.

It's worth remembering that people will only change their behaviour if they gain something positive from doing so. So HR processes must encourage and reinforce the leadership behaviours you need.

Here are a couple of examples of changes my clients made to support leadership in their organisations.

One client recognised that leaders must be involved in decision making if they were to develop leadership skills. And they needed the opportunity to share their opinions in a safe environment. As part of the development programme, we created a forum for employees to be part of the dialogue related to strategy and goals. We also provided employees with the opportunity to lead projects and strategic priorities. And we made sure that leaders took part in coaching and mentoring to enhance their impact on the culture.

Another client wanted to encourage greater collaboration among his leadership team. As CEO of the organisation, he was disappointed that they raised concerns with him.

'They should talk to each other,' he lamented, 'not just me.'

Then he came up with a great solution. He didn't make a speech. He didn't send out memos. He didn't retrain them all. He didn't print posters and hang them in the offices. Instead, he rearranged the meeting room so there was no board table, placing the chairs in a circle so the leadership team members were facing one another as well as him.

If you want your employees to talk with one another, knock down the walls. If they sit in ten different countries, use Skype and a video camera. Keep them permanently attached to their computer so there's no set-up time. Do what you can to make it easier for your people to display the leadership behaviours you're looking for. It makes a world of difference.

One technique I use is called 'Redesign With Intent'. I developed it after reading *Find Your Lightbulb* by Mike Harris, the founding CEO of telephone bank First Direct and internet bank Egg.[3] In the book, he tells a story about his mother being the greatest critic of his telephone banking venture. She gave him a whole list of reasons why telephone banking wouldn't work.

'People hate using the telephone. They hate getting passed from one department to another. They hate having to repeat the same story over and again.'

Her comments inspired him to create several statements to guide the design of the service, such as 'We will answer the phone within three rings' and 'If a customer has to be transferred to another associate, the customer information

---

3   Mike Harris (2008), *Find Your Lightbulb. How to Make Millions from Apparently Impossible Ideas.*

will be transferred with the call so they will not have to repeat themselves'.

I now take a similar approach with my clients to help them (re)design their processes with intent, and you can use it too. Write down all the obstacles that get in the way of leadership in your company. Give as many 'reasons why not' in as much detail as possible.

Now go through the list using judgement and intuition. Pick the intelligent insights that seem valid and important to you. Then produce statements of intent that say what you are going to do to deal with the issues raised.

If you want to develop a culture of leadership, expect and accept potential obstacles.

Summary

In this chapter, we've discussed five things that great companies do to help create a culture of leadership throughout the organisation. We know that we need to give leaders a clear purpose and take steps to create a movement around that purpose. We've learned why it's important to make leadership everyone's responsibility and how to recognise and reward leadership to achieve that. And we've discovered a technique for exploring how we can remove the obstacles and barriers from leadership.

1. Meet with a cross-section of leaders at all levels of the organisation to have an open discussion around what helps and hinders a culture of leadership. Explore these three areas: values and behaviours; HR policies and processes; and organisation structure and roles/responsibilities.

2. Prioritise, numbering them one to three, the areas that, if improved, would have the greatest impact on the culture of the organisation.

3. Identify sub-teams to work on each of the priority areas. Work with each sub-team to 'redesign with intent' and turn the obstacles into enablers.

Make It Happen

How do you know you have won? When the energy is coming the other way and when your people are visibly growing individually and as a group.

SIR JOHN HARVEY-JONES

At the start of this book, I told you that developing your leaders is critical if you want to grow a high-tech company. I hope that you've come to agree with that. It's something every business, large or small, needs to invest in. If you want to realise the full potential of your company, then realise the full potential of your people. And that takes skilled, confident leaders.

Now the context is clear, mastery of the six components of the LEADER system is within your reach. Mastery means that you and the leadership team have implemented each component effectively.

However, each individual component is not as important as the whole. The LEADER system recognises that leadership development is a strategic business issue. You cannot address it by itself, so LEADER takes a systemic approach to developing leaders for the organisation and what the business is trying to achieve.

Leadership development is not a quick fix. You're unlikely to see immediate improvements, but that doesn't mean you're not making progress. You're preparing your company for the future, and that is invaluable.

Be patient with the process. It's encouraging to think you can complete the Level exercise in Month 1. In Month 2, you will have envisaged future success and defined the skills and behaviours your leaders will need. In Month 3, you will have assessed all the key people, completed a People Review and drawn up Development Plans for everyone. And so on. Following this logic, by Month 7 everyone will be taking collective responsibility for leadership in the organisation.

That would be great, wouldn't it? But my experience tells me it's not always realistic. Each company moves forward at its own pace. The main thing is that you're continually making progress.

One controlling factor of how fast you can move is the current state of the company. How many people are in it? It takes longer to turn a large ship than a small one. A 1,000-person organisation is going to take longer to change than a 250-person organisation.

Put in place what you've learned

If you haven't done so already, register for the free bonus material at www.antoinetteoglethorpe.com/grow-your-geeks-resources. You'll get access to extra resources, information on leadership development, new tools and approaches. There is also a private Facebook group where you can ask questions of me and the Grow Your Geeks community.

Next, work through the LEADER system with your leadership team. Make sure the components are in place before you start working through the organisation.

Level. The reason we start here is because it makes the business case for investing in development and gets everyone on board. First you need to complete the fact-finding exercise so you know what numbers you have and what numbers you still need to find. Then have a one-to-one discussion with each leadership team member to find out what's important to them and fill any gaps in your fact-finding. That should give you the information you need to build a business case and get the leadership team's buy-in and commitment to invest in leadership development.

If you need help in implementing this component, review the material in Chapter Two.

Envisage. Once you've completed your Level activity, move on to Envisage. The Envisage component involves analysing the organisation strategy, allowing you to envisage the leadership roles, skills and behaviours that you need to deliver it.

Gather all available information on the business strategy then schedule a one-day strategy meeting with the leadership team. Review the organisation strategy, identifying the pivotal roles that will be critical for success. Complete the Future Perfect activity to identify what leaders will be doing and how they will behave when the company has achieved what it's set out to achieve. You can then analyse the vision to define the leadership skills and behaviours that you need.

Need some help in carrying this out? Look back at Chapter Three to learn more about the Envisage component.

Assess. The Assess component has two sides to it – the organisation perspective and the employee perspective. I recommend you address the employee perspective first. Provide every leadership team member with the opportunity to have a career conversation. It can be with the CEO. It can be with another member of the leadership team. Or it can be with an external coach or mentor. Then schedule a leadership team meeting to complete a People Review focused on the leaders and their direct reports. Have an honest conversation about how Ready, Willing and Able each one feels in their respective roles. Identify potential successors and future leaders, assessing their readiness, willingness and ability too. Then identify the development support they need to make progress.

If you need help with this component, refer to Chapters Four and Five for more information.

Develop. Now's the time to put the priority development areas for each individual, agreed in the People Review, into practice. The first step is a productive development planning conversation with the person concerned. The actions may involve changes to their job role and assignments to provide them with the needed opportunities, so you may wish to access support through coaches and mentors. And you may need to design or source formal training through workshops, programmes and other means.

If you want to learn more about how to put workplace challenges at the heart of the learning, re-read Chapter Six.

Embed. As you source and design the development activities, do so with an awareness of the need to:

- Inspire the desire
- Inform and reform

❯ Show they know

❯ Try and apply

❯ Review and re-do.

Review Chapter Seven if you want to remind yourself of the Embed model.

Reinforce. It will become clear that some aspects of the culture will need to change if you wish to support new leadership behaviours in the workplace. Audit your organisation practices to identify which hinder the developments you're trying to create. Meet with leaders to identify improvements that will enable leadership in the workplace.

Learn more about how to develop a culture of leadership in Chapter Eight.

Whether you implement all the ideas in this book or just a couple, take action and make it happen. At the very least, carry out a fact finding mission and identify the level of your current leadership development. That will tell you where you're starting from and help you decide where you can have the most impact. There is a saying that there are three kinds of people: those who make things happen, those who watch things happen, and those who ask, 'What happened?' If you are going to be successful in growing a high-tech company, you need to be in the first category.

Please email me with your results or to ask for advice. I answer all emails to antoinette@antoinetteoglethorpe. com personally. And I'd love to hear about your successes implementing the ideas in this book.

Grow Your Geeks. Grow your company.

The time for geeks has come.

References

Introduction

1. KPMG (Dec 2015), 'Tech Monitor'
2. Culture Amp (2016), 'New Tech – Benchmark Report'

Chapter One

1. Bersin (2010), 'Talent Management Factbook'
2. McKinsey (2001), 'War for Talent Studies'
3. Watson Wyatt (2005), 'Human Capital Index'
4. Deloitte (2014), 'Global Human Capital Trends 2014: Engaging the 21st Century Workforce'
5. Gallup (2012), 'State of the Global Workplace: Employee Engagement Insights for Business Leaders Worldwide'
6. Culture Amp (2015), New Tech Benchmark Report.

Chapter Two

1. Deloitte (2012), 'The Leadership Premium. How companies win the confidence of investors'
2. Economic Intelligence Unit (2014), 'The C-Suite Imperative'

Chapter Three

1. McKinsey (2014), 'Why Leadership Development Programs Fail'

2. Paul Z. Jackson, Mark McKergow (2007), *The Solutions Focus: Making Coaching and Change SIMPLE*

3. Center for Creative Leadership and Tata Management Training Center (2008), 'Developing Future Leaders for High-Growth Indian Companies'

Chapter Four

1. Corporate Executive Board (2005), 'Improving the Odds of Success for High-Potential Programmes'

2. Corporate Executive Board (2005), 'Realizing the Full Potential of Rising Talent: A Quantitative Analysis of the Identification and Development of High-potential'

3. Culture Amp (2015), New Tech Benchmark Report.

Chapter Five

1. CIPD (2010), 'Creating an Engaged Workforce'

2. Center for American Progress (2012), 'There Are Significant Business Costs to Replacing Employees'

3. Department for Business, Innovation and Skills (2013), 'Adult Career Decision-Making: Qualitative Research'

Chapter Six

1. Robert Gandossy, Marc Effron (2004), *Leading the Way: Three Truths from the Top Companies for Leaders*

2. Center for Creative Leadership (2014), 'Blended Learning for Leadership: The CCL Approach'

3. Ashridge Business School (2009), 'Developing the Global Leader of Tomorrow'

4. Center for Creative Leadership (2014), 'Blended Learning for Leadership: The CCL Approach'

5. Christina A Douglas (1997), *Formal Mentoring Programs in Organizations: An Annotated Bibliography*

6. Source: Yellowbrick

7. Towards Maturity (2010), 'Accelerating Performance – Towards Maturity 2010–2011 Benchmark'

8. Bersin & Associates Research Bulletin (2012), 'Integrated Talent Management: A Roadmap for Success'

Chapter Seven

1. B. J. Fogg (2014), 'Top 10 Mistakes in Behavior Change'

2. Daniel H. Pink (2010), *Drive: The Surprising Truth About What Motivates Us*

3. Accenture (2010), 'Developing Tomorrow's Talent: A girl, a blog and 30 days to business impact'

4. Marshall Goldsmith and Mark Reiter (2015), *Triggers: Creating Behavior That Lasts – Becoming the Person You Want to Be*

Chapter Eight

1. Robert B. Cialdini (2007), *Influence: The Psychology of Persuasion*

2. Daniel H. Pink (2010), *Drive: The Surprising Truth About What Motivates Us*

3. Mike Harris (2008), *Find Your Lightbulb. How to Make Millions from Apparently Impossible Ideas*

Acknowledgements

There are many people to whom I owe a sincere debt of gratitude.

Without the inspiration of **Daniel Priestley,** this book would still be in my head rather than on paper.

Without the creativity of **Rikki Bhatia,** it would have had a much more boring title.

Every time I look at the front cover of the book, I will remember the managers at **BravoSolution** who came up with the original concept behind the design. Thank you, **Alisa Matterson, Andrew Heywood, Arlene Walker, Emily Chandler, Matt O'Connor, Shreya Shah and Steve Harrison.**

Writing a book while running a business is not easy. I've been able to do both only thanks to the help and support of my wonderful PA, **Anne Williams.** You are truly the lynch pin that holds my business together.

Several people generously took the time to read the book in its early stages and give me invaluable feedback. Thank you, **David Oglethorpe, David Halliday, Jim McLaughlin, Ian Brodie, Katherine Wildman.**

Even more people provided their feedback and encouraging comments prior to publication. Thank you, **Mark Taylor, Abigail East, Rikki Bhatia, Justin Souter, John Fallou, Jane Turner, Richard Inman, Ruth Bowen, Amanda Robinson, Bernice Leppard** and **Sue Holly-Rodway.**

Still more people helped in the final stages to get it to the point where it could be published and launched. Thank you, **Lucy McCarraher** and **Joe Gregory** at **Rethink Press, Sapna Pieroux of Innervisions ID** and **Andre Marcos of Vercov.**

Last but not least, I'd like to thank all of you whom I have learned from over the years. So, thank you to my colleagues, clients, associates and partners, and the members of my mastermind groups. This book wouldn't exist without you.

The Author

Antoinette Oglethorpe is an International Talent Management and Leadership Development Consultant. She started her career at P&G, where she quickly realised she preferred developing people to washing powder.

Since then, she has developed leaders for some of the most successful organisations in the world, including P&G, Accenture and XL Group. But her real passion lies with fast-growing, high-tech companies. Antoinette's vision is for these companies to realise the leadership potential of their people so together they can create the future.

A defining moment of Antoinette's career was when she helped start up Avanade, a joint venture between Accenture and Microsoft. As International Learning Director, she played a key role in developing the people needed to grow the organisation.

And they did just that. Avanade grew to 1,200 employees in its first year.

Antoinette is a Chartered Fellow of the CIPD and a member of the Association for Coaching. She has written for CIPD Management ToolClicks, Coaching at Work and the HR Gazette; she speaks about leadership development at international conferences and events; and she hosts the Talent Development Mastery podcast on iTunes.

Contact her through:

Website: www.antoinetteoglethorpe.com

LinkedIn: uk.linkedin.com/in/antoinetteoglethorpe

Twitter: @antoinetteog

Facebook: www.facebook.com/AntoinetteOglethorpe